# NIGHTMARE IN HOLMES COUNTY
## SECOND EDITION

PATRICK MEECHAN

BEYOND THE FRAY
Publishing

BEYOND THE FRAY
Publishing

# ACKNOWLEDGMENTS

Thank you to everyone who helped make this book possible through your faithfulness, prayers and hard work.

Mom – Thank you for all your prayers and for giving me a solid Christian foundation.

Lory and Matt – Thank you for your prayers and help in many situations.

Paul and Linda Villanueva – Thanks for your prayers, support and all you've done for me.

Angie Swartzentruber – Thank you for your prayers and spiritual support during my nightmare.

Christian Ervin – Thank you for your friendship and hard work in designing the cover.

Dennis Swartzentruber – Thank you for being willing to share the secret of the haunting, as well as helping pray for my deliverance.

Thank you to my brother John as well as friends and family who helped me move to and from Holmes County.

Thank you to my dear pets Moses, Zoe, Pepper, Maggie, Copper, Pinky, Chloe, Phoebe, Priscilla, Aquila, and CJ.

MOST IMPORTANTLY, THANK YOU TO THE LORD JESUS CHRIST FOR YOUR LOVE, MERCY, GRACE AND PROVISION.

# FOREWORD

In late 2011, we read Patrick Meechan's first book, *220 5th Street*, and found that his story of survival within an extreme demonic haunting resonated with us, because we had been haunted and tormented by evil spirits until the power of God set us free. We first interviewed Patrick on the KAPOW Radio Show Network and found him so interesting and full of knowledge from above that we invited him to become a regular host on the network. He consistently brought forth deep insight with sound biblical doctrine. His experiences in surviving two consecutive haunted houses presented the audience with guidance and a realistic approach to deliverance from demonic entities.

So we were excited to hear about Patrick's new book, which is a prequel to his first work. Having the honor and pleasure to read it before its publication date, we devoured it. This new book, *Nightmare in Holmes County*, will deliver the suspense, thrills, and amazement that a true story of a real demonic haunting should. However, more importantly, this work presents wisdom with answers to so many questions, which simply cannot be found in other books of this genre.

There are evil entities within our sphere, targeting every individual with a plan to steal, kill, and destroy. But God also has a plan to rescue us from this evil and to reconcile us. The underlining message of this story is this, "with God all things are possible."

—Paul and Linda Villanueva, KAPOW Radio Show - Hemet, CA. January 20, 2015

# PREFACE

Imagine a nightmare in which your darkest fears are all coming true. Your life seems to spiral further and further towards hell with each passing day, yet you can't wake up. You're constantly dominated by unthinkable circumstances, as well as the paranormal, and everything you hold dear is in danger of being torn from your grip. I experienced this for nearly eight years, yet survived to share my testimony of hope with others. The story you're about to read is entirely true, but the names have been changed.

It is not my intention to glorify, nor disparage any particular ministers, ministries, or churches that I mention, but rather to simply tell the truth as it happened. I will not apologize for my liberal use of the Holy Scriptures or the name of Jesus, because this is the source through which my deliverance came. If you are willing to keep an open mind, I believe that you'll see that there's more to life than what we see with the naked eye. There's a spiritual realm more real than the physical, and I don't believe the paranormal is beyond the scope of our understanding. The truth is out there, and it's my sincere hope that through sharing my experiences, I can help point others to that truth.

# INTRODUCTION

The purpose of this book is to document my eight-year-long battle with demonic forces while living in the second-largest population of Amish in the world. While I'm certain there are many God-fearing Amish people who do not engage in witch-craft or the occult, sadly many secretly do. There were, however, even darker and more deep-rooted reasons for the haunting I was experiencing than just the local practice of witchcraft.

In the most insidious cases of haunting activity, often multiple doors have been opened to demonic spirits, allowing a multifaceted attack against those living in that environment. Such was the case in the story I'm about to share.

# CHAPTER ONE

## THE BEGINNING

*I*t all seemed like a dream come true. I never suspected at the time that it was really just the early stages of a nightmare from which I thought I'd never awaken. It was early autumn 2001, and like everyone else, my wife, Chelsea, and I were still reeling from the 9/11 attacks. On a personal level, however, things appeared to be looking up for us. We had only been married a little over two years, and we'd been living in an apartment while saving money to one day buy a piece of land in the country and build our dream home.

We'd recently spoken to a builder named Jonus Yoder, who told us he'd just noticed a piece of land that might interest us in Holmes County, Ohio. Jonus was an older man in his sixties who was born into an older order Amish family, but had left the religion when he was young. He had, however, maintained a very close relationship with the Amish, which was a wise decision, considering Holmes County is the second-largest population of Amish in the entire world. At the time, Jonus wore a very friendly veneer, which led us to believe he was a kind, grandfatherly type of individual.

Jonus took us to the land, which had just recently been put up for sale. Neither Chelsea nor I liked the fact that the property was located on a dirty gravel township road, but the land was beautiful. The six-acre plot was surrounded by Amish farms and seemed very peaceful and quiet. Somehow the sky seemed much bigger here than in eastern Tuscarawas County, where I grew up. A large creek ran just below the property and through the open fields that were directly across the road. Off in the distance stood a quaint, small Mennonite church, which made the scenery seem reminiscent of a Thomas Kinkade painting. The price was reasonable, and it all seemed too good to be true. We got the phone number posted on the For Sale sign and told Jonus we'd get back to him.

Upon arriving home, we called the seller, who turned out to be a young Amish couple named Myron and Sarah Jane Miller. They told us they'd recently bought the land, and then shortly thereafter, a family member gave them a free piece of land in Kidron, Ohio. Since they didn't need two properties, they claimed to be merely asking what they'd just paid for the six acres in Holmes County. After the phone call, Chelsea and I were definitely interested in the land.

The following Saturday evening, I arrived home from work to find the apartment empty. Chelsea wasn't home, and I had no idea where she might have gone. Figuring she'd be home soon enough, I went to the spare bedroom to unwind by playing my guitar. A short while later, Chelsea arrived home and immediately sought me out. She entered the spare bedroom with a huge grin on her face and held up the For Sale sign that had been posted at the property in Holmes County. "Your wife just negotiated a great price, and we got the land!" she proudly announced.

I was overjoyed. The thought never entered my mind that it was strange or inappropriate that she had taken control and made such a huge decision on her own, without me even being present during negotiations. To the contrary, I couldn't have been more proud of her. The Millers claimed that although they were selling the land for a little less than what they had just paid for it, they were happy to be selling so quickly. Jonus drew up a building contract, and we began the process of obtaining a mortgage, and spent the rest of 2001 joyfully anticipating the building of our dream home the following spring.

# CHAPTER TWO

## OMENS AND THE WATCHER

Things began to seem a little strange when we took the building contract to our mortgage company. Our banker, Mr. Don Peters, took one look at it, and his cheerful demeanor suddenly became agitated. "This is *not* a building contract! You go tell Jonus that he's a big boy, and he knows how to write up a *real* contract. This isn't good enough! He's omitted way too many details about how he's going to build your house and what materials he's using!"

I took the contract back to Jonus and told him the bank wanted him to redo it. He pretended to be very surprised and claimed that this was how he always wrote up the contracts. He did agree to make some minor changes, and after doing so, I took the contract back to the bank. Mr. Peters looked at it again and grumbled a bit more, but he eventually accepted it, and our loan was approved shortly thereafter.

By mid-February 2002, Jonus broke ground and began building our house. It was a very exciting time for us. Everything began taking shape quite quickly, and in what seemed like no time, the foundation was poured, the basement walls were built, and the framing of the house began.

Then on Saturday evening, March 9, the unthinkable happened. The first and second floors were completely framed, and the exterior walls were being nailed up, when a strong storm hit. Even though the walls had been strongly braced, the storm produced high winds, which completely leveled the house. All that was left was a pile of twisted wood lying on the first floor. When Jonus called us and broke the bad news, he seemed dumbfounded. "In all my years of building, I have *never* seen anything like this!" he claimed in disbelief.

Not only was the house flattened, but some of the framing had actually been driven through the plywood flooring of the first level! At the time, we considered the incident to be merely bad *luck*. After evaluating the damage, the insurance investigator said that there was nothing that could have been done differently to stop the disaster. The damaged wood was removed and auctioned off, and rebuilding began.

(It turned out that Jonus' cousin Jim Yoder had won the sealed bid auction and gotten approximately $20,000 worth of wood for less than $200. We also learned that cousin Jim was not only going to be our mailman, but was also a township trustee. An insurance investigator later told me that he believed Jonus had opened competing bids and told his cousin Jim how much to bid. The investigator then added that because there was no proof, it would be a waste of time and money trying to prosecute. On the bright side, Jonus assured us that once our house was built, Jim and the other trustees would pave the dusty gravel township road in front of our home.)

*Was the devastation of the house collapsing simply bad luck or an omen of unseen forces at work?*

AS TIME WORE ON, we began seeing another side of Jonus that was much different from the seemingly kind gentleman we'd hired. Although we had agreed that the master bathroom would have both a shower and Jacuzzi tub, we arrived at the house one day to discover that Jonus had quickly installed a standard garden-style tub. We were disappointed, but tried to show a good Christian attitude and let it slide.

7

On another occasion, Jonus threw a temper tantrum and kicked the heating and cooling crew that I had subcontracted out of the house, and wouldn't let them in to do their work. This not only caused undue tension at the building site, but also cost us more money because the heating and cooling contractor was forced to charge us for the incident because his crew had lost a day of work. It became apparent that the benevolent gentleman we'd hired to build our house seemed to be long gone, and in his place was a ruthless, mean-spirited grouch. Had he just put up a good front at first, or was he inexplicably changing the longer he worked on our house?

Other than Jonus' son Tim, the work crew was a strange bunch as well, especially a young man named Abe. Although Abe wasn't Amish, his family was, and he lived with his parents high on a hill that overlooked the part of the valley where our house sat. Abe was an awkward sort in his mid-twenties. He was single and didn't seem like the type who'd have many prospects when it came to eligible young ladies.

Over Memorial Day weekend, Chelsea and I went to the house to stain and varnish woodwork because the crew was off for the holiday. Chelsea drove separately and arrived a good forty-five minutes to an hour before I did. She went straight to the basement and started working. A short while later she heard someone enter the house and begin walking around upstairs. At first she assumed it was me, but then she began hearing a strange, haunting voice calling her name. "Chelsea, Chelsea," she heard the voice call out. She instantly knew the voice was not mine, so she thought that perhaps her father had showed up unannounced and was playing a joke on her.

"I'm down here!" she answered. She heard footsteps walk across the floor above and then descend the basement stairs. Much to Chelsea's surprise, it was not her father. It was Abe! Although she knew I'd be arriving at any minute, she felt very uncomfortable. When I arrived a short while later, Abe didn't hang around. He quickly left and returned to his parents' house. As Chelsea and I discussed the situation, it became very clear that Abe had been watching from his parents' house and had invited himself over, knowing that Chelsea was alone. This was unsettling and not something I would tolerate. I spoke to Jonus, who downplayed the incident, but agreed to have a talk with Abe.

I never made much of it back then, but several times when I went to the house alone late in the evening to finish woodwork, I would often have an uneasy feeling that I was being watched. Although I knew I was alone, the feeling was intense and very hard to shake. I tried to concentrate on praying and singing Christian songs or hymns as I worked, which seemed to help a little. I attributed the feelings to being in a large unfamiliar house that was located seemingly in the middle of nowhere.

One July afternoon, I stopped by the house to see how the construction was coming along. I'd often stop on my way to work and bring cold refreshments to the crew, because the hot Ohio summer days could seem merciless. On this particular afternoon, my visit coincided with the crew's lunch break. They were all resting in the garage, and I noticed that Abe was acting stranger than usual. He sat silently on a cooler against the wall, with a blank stare on his face. Something seemed to be eating at him. As I was making small talk with Jonus, Abe suddenly interjected, "There was a man here last night!"

Upon hearing this, I remembered that Chelsea; her best friend, Sarah; and Sarah's new boyfriend, Tom, had stopped by the previous evening to see the house. "Yeah, that was just Chelsea and a couple of friends who came to see the house," I explained.

"No, that's not what I'm talking about!" Abe responded slowly. He swallowed hard and then continued, "Last evening before dark, I had to take my car over to Sim's Garage to have some work done on it. I took a shortcut down your road, and when I got in front of your house, I saw a man hiding in the high grass by the property line. He was watching your house, and he was *very* scary looking! I had to walk home after I dropped my car off, and I was so scared that I went the long way just so I wouldn't have to see him again!"

I didn't know what to make of Abe's story. It certainly appeared as though *he* believed what he was saying, but I had to question in my own mind if he was mentally competent. If he'd really taken the long way home after seeing the strange man hiding in the grass, he would have walked several miles out of his way just to avoid passing the man again on the lonely township road.

"Well, I'm getting a security system installed, and I have guns. If anyone makes me or Chelsea feel threatened, they'll get themselves shot!" I responded.

"Well, that's right," Jonus chirped up. "That's how it should be. A man's gotta protect his family!"

Abe, however, didn't seem so agreeable. His expression became even more fearful as he stared at me in total silence. I later questioned Jonus about Abe's mental state, and he claimed that Abe merely had "emotional problems."

On another hot summer afternoon, I again stopped by to check the progress of the crew. It was now into August, and they were nowhere near being finished. Jonus had promised us that the house would be completed within three months, and it was now nearing six. I went to the basement, where Jonus' son Tim was working. As I was talking to Tim, I noticed that the basement wall that was located directly below the front door had a large crack from top to bottom, and the sunlight from outside was shining through. When I pointed this out to Tim, he assured me that Jonus would have all of the cracked cement blocks taken out and replaced. Later, I noticed that it *appeared* that they had indeed replaced the damaged blocks.

By September, Chelsea and I and our faithful cat Moses finally moved in. We had multiple disagreements with Jonus, and it became painfully obvious why he had written such a generic building contract. He had added many additional expenses and neglected to complete much of what he'd promised. Additionally, he'd subcontracted some of the work on the house to Amish companies who did very unsatisfactory work. For instance, the Amish craftsman Jonus hired to finish the hardwood floors in the foyer, kitchen, and dining room had applied the finish right over the top of small piles of sawdust, dirt, and long, curly, Amish beard hairs. It would have been a simple task to simply thoroughly sweep the floors first, yet he'd neglected to do so. As if that wasn't bad enough, the finish also wasn't applied evenly. I voiced my disapproval and stood my ground. We eventually settled our dispute, and Jonus was paid the fair and proper amount we'd agreed upon originally. I thought we'd just go our separate ways and put the bad blood behind us. Little did I know, however, that is not how things are done in Amish country.

# CHAPTER THREE

## THE UGLY TRUTH

*T*he fall of 2002 should have been a happy time for us. We were now living in what we thought was our dream home, but there always seemed to be a new discovery that dampened our spirits. One day, Chelsea returned home from visiting one of our few non-Amish neighbors and informed me that Abe's condition was, in fact, much worse than "emotional problems." According to our neighbor Mrs. Thompson, Abe was not only *allegedly* schizophrenic, but he was also a voyeur who had been caught on multiple occasions sneaking into homes and watching women and young girls while they bathed and dressed. Abe had avoided criminal prosecution because each family that had caught him was Amish or Mennonite and didn't believe in prosecution. This new information was exceptionally disturbing, considering that Abe had helped build our house and knew every nook and cranny. He also certainly would have had access to our keys. I was thankful we'd had a security system installed, but I also took extra precautions and changed the locks on every door.

We also discovered that just about a quarter mile down the road from our house was a strange location where it appeared that kids went to party. This area was on Amish farmland where there was a clearing just off to the side of the road. We never actually saw any kids there, but we'd often see many beer cans and bottles scattered about on the ground, and someone had painted "I love pot" on a tree there. Sometimes late at night, we'd hear strange noises that we assumed were loud music coming from that area as well.

One Sunday afternoon, while I was lifting weights in the basement, Chelsea decided to drive to Lowe's Home Improvement for some supplies. After being gone for several hours, she returned with what finally seemed like good news.

"You know that clearing up the road where the kids party?"

"Yes," I replied.

"Well, when I drove through on my way to town, I saw a little beagle just sitting there with no one around. When I came back through, over two hours later, he was still there, sitting in the *exact* same spot, like he hadn't even moved. I think someone dumped him off. If he's still there, can we get him?" she asked.

"Sure," I answered. "As soon as I finish a couple more sets, I'll come with you!"

Chelsea quickly headed out of the basement and left the house to go check on the dog. Before I could even join her, she'd returned with our new pet. He was a small, skinny beagle with a mark around his neck where a collar had once been. When he saw me, he suddenly seemed very scared, making it obvious he'd suffered abuse in his young life and probably from a man. Eventually, however, I gained his trust. We named him Copper and welcomed him to the family.

At first I figured Copper's owner had dumped him in that location and the poor little dog sat there waiting in vain for him to return. As I've gotten to know him better, however, I realized that obedience isn't one of Copper's strong points. Furthermore, Copper can't sit still for very long, as his strong sense of smell always seems to lead him off on some new investigation. Maybe there was another reason why he sat in that area, frozen, as if he was afraid to move.

I often worked evenings, and Chelsea began complaining of hearing strange noises while she was alone. I began hearing the noises as well, but I attributed them to settling or shortcuts Jonus had taken while building the house. I hated to admit it, but the noises were eerie and sinister sounding. I even joked that Jonus' craftsmanship was *so* bad that every time the wind blew, it sounded like we lived in a haunted house.

In early 2003, we hired home inspectors to come and evaluate the house, and what they discovered only added to our disappointments. Jonus had taken shortcuts we hadn't even imagined. Among other problems, we discovered that the fifteen-foot-tall brick fireplace in our living room had absolutely no support under it in the basement, and it was beginning to move. Without supports, the entire hearth could give way and crash through to the basement, possibly killing someone!

Our new house needed major repair work, and it was going to be expensive. Even the large crack that went from bottom to top on the front basement wall had reappeared! We hired an attorney who also happened to be the Holmes County assistant prosecutor. He sent a few letters to Jonus' attorney, but this really got us nowhere. Our attorney's efforts accomplished nothing, and his fees only added to the stress we were feeling. He eventually told us, "Well, Jonus isn't cooperating, so think it over and let me know if you want to sue him."

We thought it over and realized that we had no choice *but* to sue. I made several futile attempts to contact our attorney, but he never returned my calls. I lost all faith and trust in him and began wondering just how much power the Amish *really* had in Holmes County. Although Jonus technically had left the Amish religion, he was still accepted by them, and he provided work for them by subcontracting his building jobs.

It certainly was clear that although our attorney was happy to take a large amount of money from us in fees, he really had no intention of filing a lawsuit on our behalf. Disgruntled, we dropped everything and hired a contractor we knew from our church to complete the repairs. By late spring 2003, his work was complete, and everything was finally how it should have been originally.

After the repairs were completed, *most* of the strange noises stopped, but subtle inexplicable events began occurring. One such event happened almost immediately after the repairs had been completed. Just off the living room was our laundry room, which contained our washer and dryer, a utility tub, a closet, and the door that led to the garage. This room was where we kept Moses' food and water dishes and the litter box. Late one evening I was in this room feeding Moses, when suddenly for no reason, the closed dryer door sprang open all by itself. I found this very strange considering the manner in which a dryer door latches shut, but I tried not to dwell on it. Around this same time, Chelsea began traveling frequently for work, leaving me alone in the house. I'd occasionally experience that eerie, familiar feeling of being watched, but I would quickly dismiss it from my mind.

We got our closest neighbor that year when Abe's older brother Eli built a house just over the hill from us. Eli was Amish, and he ran a sawmill behind his house. Just at the edge of his property was the strange clearing where we suspected kids held their drinking parties. The parties seemed to stop, however, after Eli moved in. Although Eli seemed friendly enough, there was something about him I didn't quite trust.

There was one bright spot that spring. One night when I went out to feed Copper, I found an adorable female Rottweiler puppy hiding beside the house. We named her Maggie and accepted her into the family. I later discovered that like Copper, Maggie had been dumped and wandered to our house. I will never understand how anyone could just dump an animal, but I was thankful to have the new pets. Maggie quickly assumed her role as protector of the family.

In June our family grew yet again when Chelsea's mother's barn cat had kittens. We chose a tiny calico kitten and named her Zoe. She had a lot of personality and really livened up the home. Eventually, the pets would have great significance in the paranormal activity that was slowly beginning to escalate.

# CHAPTER FOUR

## GROUNDWORK FOR A CURSE

As time wore on, we began having problems with the Amish. They thought nothing of coming on to our property as if it were theirs. I didn't take kindly to this, as I respected their property and expected the same from them. They would cross our property for hunting without even considering asking permission. One night, while several Amish men were trespassing while coon hunting, I'd had enough. I approached and asked if I could help them. Two of the younger men, who appeared to be in their twenties, shined a bright light in my face and said, "We're coon hunting!" in an arrogant tone.

Unbeknownst to me, the older man with them was none other than Abe's father. I had long since grown weary of the hypocrisy of my Amish neighbors, and I decided it was time to speak my mind. I made it very clear to them that they were trespassing and I wouldn't tolerate it. While walking them to the truck where their driver was waiting, I communicated to them, in no uncertain terms, that there would be major problems if they continued trespassing.

Although I was outnumbered three to one and they were armed, I couldn't resist standing up to them. What I didn't know at the time was that even if the Amish back down when you're face-to-face, they *are* going to get even with you sooner or later. Looking back, maybe it would have been wiser to back down or look the other way. After the incident I called the sheriff and filed a complaint, thinking that it was the right thing to do.

As if the trespassing wasn't annoying enough, other problems emerged as well. We'd decided to rent our fields to a Mennonite farmer who wanted to grow hay. He promised he'd pay for the rental of the acreage before the end of the year. I soon discovered that although he paid all the Amish land owners in a timely manner, he continually neglected to pay us until well into the following year, and only after I made *several* phone calls asking for the money. I heard rumors that if someone butted heads with the Amish, they'd be marked and suffer some level of shunning or even retaliation from the Amish community. I was beginning to believe it was true! I also learned that drug trafficking, incest, and child molestation were prevalent among the Amish, but it was all done secretly.

Coincidentally, in addition to the Amish nuisances, subtle paranormal incidents also began increasing. I started noticing strange shadows out of the corner of my eyes, but when I'd look, nothing would be there. Not knowing what to make of it, I spoke to my pastor, and he told me that he'd also experienced this before. He then offered some advice. "It might be a spirit," he said. "But do yourself a favor and go get your eyes checked. If your eyes are ok, then it might be demons."

I took my pastor's advice and made an appointment with my optometrist, Dr. Joseph. While he was giving me an exam, I decided to share my strange experiences.

"So what's the deal when you keep seeing things out of the corner of your eyes, but when you look, nothing's there?"

"Are you seeing shadows or flashes of light?" he asked.

"Shadows," I answered.

"Well, if you see lights, you may have a detached retina. If you are seeing shadows, however, you are either suffering from a type of stroke, or you are seeing spirits," he answered. The examination confirmed that I had nothing wrong with my eyes that would explain the strange shadows I was seeing, and I was not suffering from any type of stroke.

Late one night, as I was getting ready to retire for the evening, I went to the laundry room and topped off Moses and Zoe's food dish. As I turned to put the bag of cat food back into the closet, I saw Zoe rush into the room and go right to her dish and begin eating.

"How cute," I thought to myself.

I put the cat food away and exited the room, leaving Zoe alone with her snack. I walked through the dining room and foyer and turned to go upstairs to the bedroom, when to my surprise, I saw Zoe sitting on the top step, looking down at me.

"What in the world? That must have been Moses in the laundry room!" I reassured myself. But I was certain it was Zoe!

I continued up the stairs, passed Zoe, and opened the bedroom door, only to find Moses sleeping on the bed with Chelsea! The next day I told Chelsea what had happened, all the while hoping she wouldn't think I was crazy.

"Don't even tell me that!" she quipped. "There have been times when I'm home alone, and I'm in the basement using the elliptical, and I'll swear I see Moses run past, out of the corner of my eye. Then I'll remember that we don't allow him in the basement, and he's upstairs, and the basement door is shut!"

This was not welcome news, but I was happy that she believed me. I wondered if there were other experiences Chelsea wasn't sharing, considering that she hadn't shared this until I'd first related my experience. I wondered what could be the cause of this activity. Considering we'd built the house, how could it be haunted?

Over time, Chelsea's behavior was changing too. There were times I actually felt that she hated me. Her attitude towards me was occasionally hostile, and at times she even violently attacked me. This was not entirely new behavior, however, as I'd seen hints of this lurking under the surface in the past, but not to this degree. Once during an argument, she ran across the room and hit me in the chest with an open hand and, in one motion, ripped open my shirt and tore off my gold cross necklace and threw it across the room. These violent episodes were not frequent, but they did happen multiple times. Each time, I would simply hold her arms down to stop her from hitting me, and talk calmly until her violent rage subsided. Sadly, she knew she could get away with this behavior because no matter what, I'd never hit her. I never even swore at her, not even once. I did all I could to be a Godly, Christian husband. At the time, I didn't recognize her behavior as physical and mental abuse, and I didn't tell anyone about it. I guess it's hard for a man to see that he's the victim of abuse at the hands of a woman.

Early one Saturday morning, in June 2004, we received a terrible phone call. Chelsea's best friend, Sarah, and her now husband, Tom, were in a horrible motorcycle accident. They both sustained multiple life-threatening injuries, including torn aortas! Although very few people survive a torn aorta, many fervent prayers were offered up on their behalf, and God was merciful. Both survived, but their recoveries were long and grueling. Chelsea began spending many hours away from home to be with her friend. I applauded her for showing support. It was the Christian thing to do, I thought.

On Saturday afternoon, October 16, we received a visit from an Amish man named Isaac Raber. He explained that he lived on a farm located to the rear of our property and several fields away. He told me that he wanted to give a piece of his land to his son, but that the piece of property was landlocked because of the large creek running through it. Instead of building a bridge over the creek, Isaac asked me to *give* him a right-of-way that stretched the entire length of our property so he could install a lane to the landlocked field.

"I'm sorry, Isaac, but I can't do that. The lane would devalue our property. I'd have to charge you for the right-of-way, and to be honest, even then it just wouldn't be worth it to us," I respectfully answered.

Isaac seemed disappointed with my answer as he left and returned home. I honestly couldn't believe he had the nerve to ask me to *give* him the right-of-way. The rest of 2004 seemed to be uneventful from what I could tell.

## CHAPTER FIVE

2005

*L*ooking back at 2005, it's clear to me now that everything had begun a slow downward spiral. When you're in the thick of things, however, it's hard to see it, and even harder to know how to stop it. Chelsea had become much more distant and was traveling more frequently for work. When she wasn't traveling, she was spending time with Sarah. I found my escape in songwriting and Bible study. Although these were good activities, I wasn't seeing the reality of the situation. My marriage was slowly crumbling.

I continued having subtle paranormal experiences, such as seeing the strange shadows, but I had no idea what to do or how significant they really were. Although Chelsea scared easily and had never watched horror movies or any television programs regarding the paranormal, we both started watching *A Haunting* and *Ghost Hunters*. We didn't get into deep discussion about it, but we both knew something was wrong in our home. In the beginning, she'd only watch the shows with me and never when she was alone.

One afternoon, while I was home alone and working in our office, I had the curtains wide open, letting the bright sunlight in, when suddenly I saw a shadow move across the wall, exactly like what I'd see if someone walked across the front porch, blocking the light coming in the window. I looked out the windows and saw no one, so I went immediately to answer the door. I opened the door and stepped out on the front porch, but no one was there. Perplexed, I went back inside. Approximately five minutes later, as I was in the kitchen, thinking about this strange incident, the doorbell rang. I answered the door to find Isaac Raber standing on the porch.

"How long have you been here, Isaac?" I asked.

"I just pulled up," he answered while pointing at his bike, which now sat at the end of the sidewalk.

"About five minutes ago, I saw a shadow go across the windows of my office, just like when someone walks across the porch. That wasn't you?"

"No, it wasn't me. I just got here," he assured me. He then proceeded to ask me *again* to give him a right-of-way for the lane, and again I kindly refused.

"Isaac, that lane would have to be the entire length of my property, and it would devalue my land. I'm sorry, but I can't do that," I answered. Once again Isaac's disappointment was obvious as he left.

Shortly thereafter, Isaac and his family began acting as though I *had* given them a right-of-way on our property. Several times we caught him or his adult daughter walking right through our yard as though it was theirs. When we'd ask them what they were doing, they'd answer as though I was ignorant for questioning them. I decided to have a stern discussion with Isaac and explained to him that I didn't trespass on his land, and I wouldn't tolerate him or his family trespassing on mine. He acted as though he understood and agreed to stop.

As if the situation with Isaac's family wasn't enough of a concern, I'd also heard more and more stories about Abe's voyeurism over the past couple of years, and now I was noticing him walking by our house frequently. One afternoon, while mowing the lawn, I saw him slowly walking on the road in front of the house, so I stopped the mower and approached him.

"Abe, I heard a rumor that you like to sneak into people's houses and hide and spy on them. Is that true?" I asked.

"Yes," he proudly answered. As if his voyeuristic behavior itself wasn't odd enough, the unashamed tone of his voice was even more troubling.

"Well, here's the deal, Abe. If you ever come on my property, I will prosecute you for trespassing. If you ever come in my house, you will leave in a body bag. Do I make myself clear?" I asked.

"Yes," Abe slowly replied while giving me a blank stare.

"You've been other people's problem, and they didn't take care of things. If you become my problem, I will!" I warned.

Abe then walked on down the road. I didn't like giving such a stern warning, but I believe a voyeur, especially one who has progressed to the point of entering homes, is a very dangerous person. Additionally, it was clear that Abe had no intentions of changing, and he showed no remorse for his actions. It was my sincere hope that my warning would deter any future problems. The last thing I wanted was Chelsea living in fear of a perverted and possibly psychotic neighbor.

In the fall of 2005, my pastor asked me for the third time to teach an adult Sunday school class, so I finally agreed. The class was mostly college-age individuals, but was open to those up to age forty. It was set to begin in January of 2006, and I looked forward to teaching, and took the position very seriously. I decided I'd get back to the basics and teach straight from the Bible.

# CHAPTER SIX

## THE UNRAVELING

*I*n January, I enthusiastically began teaching Sunday school, but within two months, it became painfully obvious that the students did *not* want to hear about repentance, holiness, or the fear of the Lord. One of the most disrespectful students happened to also be the worship leader in the church. One morning in class, he arrogantly proclaimed, "I'm only here to tear down what you're trying to do!"

I had also heard from multiple sources that he was attending keg parties and womanizing, so it was obvious why he was causing problems. A short while later, the associate pastor asked me to have lunch with him, stating that he needed to talk to me. Over lunch, he basically told me that instead of praying and asking God what *He* wanted me to teach, I should just ask the class what they wanted to be taught. With that, it was obvious that the worship leader had complained about what I was teaching, and now the church wanted me to coddle sinners who didn't want to change. Disgusted, I resigned and left the church. The problem now was that I had no idea where to go, and I needed a church family more than ever.

During the time that I was teaching, I was also trying desperately to understand what was going on with Chelsea. Because she was in the class, I had hoped that maybe she would grow spiritually as well, which would strengthen our marriage. To the contrary, it was plain to see that she was slowly backsliding further and further from the truth. By spring 2006, her hostility towards me had increased substantially, and there was absolutely no intimacy in the marriage. She was away on business trips more than ever, and now Sarah, who was also now having marriage problems, was tagging along with her. As her behavior became more peculiar, I began wondering if the sleep disturbances Chelsea suffered, for as long as I'd known her, might be somehow relevant. During sleep, she would grind her teeth and also frequently have night terrors, in which she'd suddenly awaken and sit up gasping in fear, but have no idea why. She also had an abnormal fear of dolls, which I now suspected was related.

One day, I also noticed that Chelsea had moved the large family Bible from the coffee table in our living room to a bookshelf in our home office, where it was out of the way and out of sight. This Bible had been a wedding gift and had *always* been displayed prominently on our coffee table. Now, however, it seemed she was either ashamed or couldn't stand the sight of it.

On a Sunday afternoon in May, I was once again in the basement working out while Chelsea used the elliptical. My exercise bench was positioned a few feet from the basement wall, just in front of the large crack that had once again reappeared directly below the front door. Although Chelsea was wearing headphones, I turned on the television just in time to hear Carrie Underwood sing "Jesus Take the Wheel," which I'd always found to be an uplifting song.

I was bench-pressing, so I warmed up and did my first set with 225 pounds and then decided to do my second set with 275 pounds. I lay back on the bench and meditated on the words of the song for a few seconds and then started my set. As I lifted the weight off the bench, it suddenly felt like it was at least 400 pounds! Thankfully, there were spotter stands built into the bench, because the weight felt so heavy that I couldn't even lower it slowly! As the weight came crashing down onto the spotter stands, I felt a massive pain in my left shoulder and pectoral muscle. I went immediately to the hospital and later got an MRI, which showed that I had sustained a partial tear of my left pectoral muscle. The pain was excruciating, and within two days, much of my left arm had turned completely black. I found it curious that 275 pounds could do so much damage, and I wondered what could have caused the weight to suddenly feel so much heavier than usual. My muscle hadn't torn until the barbell had reached the spotter stand at the bottom of the range of motion, so the sudden sensation of the weight drastically increasing could not be attributed to the muscle tearing.

As if this all wasn't disturbing enough, while I was leaving the emergency room on the day of the accident, Chelsea and I were walking to the car when I noticed a very elderly and feeble gentleman walking across the parking lot in a strange manner. His knees seemed to be buckled as he walked, and he was holding his arms in a strange manner across his chest. At first, his gait seemed so strange that I assumed he was crippled, but just after getting into the car, I realized he was actually having a heart attack. As Chelsea was driving slowly through the parking lot towards the exit, I looked in the mirror just in time to see him collapse.

"Stop! That man is having a heart attack!" I exclaimed. Chelsea ignored me.

"Stop. He collapsed! Let me out!" I insisted.

As if I hadn't said a word and showing no regard for the ailing elderly man, Chelsea drove right out of the parking lot and continued down the road. I couldn't comprehend how she could be so coldhearted.

"That man is probably dying right now! Why didn't you stop? I would have gotten him help and prayed with him!"

"He's at the hospital. They'll come out and help him," she flippantly answered.

Chelsea's behavior was so strange that it seemed as if she was actually happy that the elderly stranger was suffering and quite possibly dying. She made it clear that she was defiant against anything I said. Chelsea knew me very well and knew that my greatest concern was that man's salvation, because he appeared to be close to death. None of that mattered to *her* anymore, however. Where was the woman I married? Was that person ever real, or was she always this hateful and just covered it well?

Chelsea had been with me many times when I shared my faith with people. On several occasions when I'd seen someone asking for money on the street, I'd buy food for them and then slip in a Bible tract. She knew I was concerned about that man's soul, and she didn't want me to have the opportunity to share Jesus with him. I hoped and prayed that he was either already a Christian, or that someone else prayed with him.

I had a sickening feeling that quite possibly God had allowed my accident so I would be at the hospital to help and pray with that man. Since Chelsea was *playing* devil's advocate, however, I didn't get the opportunity. The thought crossed my mind that she might not be *playing* at all, but rather had actually *become* his advocate. At times it certainly seemed that way.

After that incident, Chelsea's behavior became even colder by the day. Although I'd sustained a serious and painful injury, it was obvious that she couldn't care less. I felt like I was married to a total stranger. Even her taste in music drastically changed, and she began downloading vulgar and profane songs to her mp3 player. We began getting hang-up calls late at night as well, and often she wouldn't talk on the phone if I was in the same room. I then noticed that the seats in her car would be adjusted differently than normal and slightly reclined.

One evening shortly before 11:00 p.m., as I was about to go outside to feed Maggie and Copper, I noticed that her brand-new car was *covered* in scratches. I went to the bedroom and informed her of my discovery, but she wasn't the least bit concerned. Instead, she was only upset that I'd awakened her. She demanded we start marriage counseling, to which I readily agreed, but it became evident very quickly that the counseling was merely a charade.

We found a Christian counselor in Canton, Ohio, and began seeing him weekly. One evening during a counseling session, I mentioned that as long as I'd known Chelsea, she'd suffered from teeth grinding and night terrors. He explained to both of us that these were symptoms of post-traumatic stress disorder and repressed memories of traumatic events. I wanted more than anything to help her work through whatever trauma she'd suffered, but I couldn't force her to deal with anything against her will. I then shared with the counselor that Chelsea's recent behavior was also indicative of marital infidelity.

Later that evening, after we returned home, I had a very strange and unnerving experience. As Chelsea and I were in our living room, watching an episode of *A Haunting*, I was lying on the couch and she was seated on the love seat, which put her behind me and out of my range of vision. Suddenly, I felt as though Chelsea's presence left the room. This is difficult to explain, but at first I knew she was in the room with me and I felt her presence. Then suddenly, it felt as though I was alone. I hadn't heard her get up and walk out of the room, so I asked her a question to see if she'd answer me. There was dead silence. I asked the question again, and still there was no answer. After I repeated the question a third time without a response, I turned to look, and found her sitting upright with her head tilted back as though she was looking towards the room's vaulted ceiling. Her eyes and mouth were wide open, and it was as if she was in a trance, with her expression resembling a terrifying death stare!

"Chelsea, are you ok?" I asked. Her head jerked, and suddenly she snapped out of the trance.

"Yes, I'm ok. *Why?*" she responded in a condescending tone.

"Because I asked you a question three times and you didn't answer me," I explained.

"I didn't even hear you," she responded as a confused expression came across her face.

I have never had an experience quite like that before, or since, and I have no explanation for it. As if her behavior itself wasn't strange enough, the fact that I felt her presence leave the room was quite disturbing. It seemed as though her spirit had left, but her body was still there. Part of me believed that the incident was somehow related to what the counselor had shared with us earlier that evening, regarding post-traumatic stress and repressed memories of traumatic events.

I have also, however, spoken to several people who formerly were involved in the occult, who told me that the incident seems indicative that Chelsea might have, without my knowledge, become involved in soul travel or astral projection. Astral projection is a practice in which a person's spirit, through demonic power, can leave their body and visit other places without physically going there. Although I was left with more questions, one thing was certain: Chelsea had deep, dark secrets.

The paranormal activity began escalating even more as well during this time. Besides the elusive shadows, the television now began changing channels by itself, and at times the lights in the house would flicker for no apparent reason. I tried to talk to Chelsea about these strange incidents, but she downplayed them as though I was accusing her of being the source of the activity.

"Well, it's probably just because *you* watch *Ghost Hunters*!" she argued.

"No, I don't think that has anything to do with it. I don't understand why, but I think the devil is attacking our marriage," I tried to explain.

One morning when my alarm clock rang, I tried everything to turn it off, but to no avail. I pushed every button and flipped every lever, but nothing turned it off, or even switched from the clock's loud buzzer to the radio's alarm function.

"Come here, Chelsea. I want you to see this for yourself. See if you can explain this or shut it off," I said.

She confidently marched into the room and grabbed the alarm clock, fully expecting she'd easily turn it off and make a fool of me. She then also tried everything, flipping every lever and pushing every button, but nothing shut the alarm off. Eventually, she reached over and unplugged it and stood there dumbfounded.

"Ok, *that is weird!*" she agreed.

Chelsea's hostility towards me increased exponentially as time wore on, and I began finding strange notes that she wrote to herself, which led me to suspect she was getting legal counsel for a divorce. The notes detailed our conversations, arguments, and even the fights she'd start with me. Because the counseling was accomplishing nothing, I decided to try a female Christian counselor, hoping Chelsea might open up to her. This also proved useless.

One day, while driving, I decided to call the counselor and tell her about the paranormal activity and Chelsea's changes in behavior. The counselor totally scoffed at the idea of paranormal activity or that demons are even active in the world today. This was extremely frustrating considering she was **supposed** to be a "Christian" counselor, and I was paying her $120 per session.

"Listen, if your channels are changing by themselves, I can explain that. If you have a satellite, your neighbors are probably using their remote to change their channels, and it is affecting your satellite and making your channels change," she argued in a contemptuous tone. (I have never experienced this, and no one I've known has ever claimed to have anything like this happen either!)

"Well, my neighbors are Amish, so they don't have satellites, but none of them live close enough to me for that to happen anyway," I explained.

"Oh," she responded and then hesitated as though she didn't know what to say next. She waited a few moments to regroup and then continued, "Well, demons *were* in the Bible, but they're not active in the world nowadays."

"Really? Where's that in the Bible? It never says any such thing! Demons were active then and they're active now," I countered.

Suddenly, a semi tractor-trailer drove straight into my lane of traffic as if I wasn't even there! I quickly swerved and went completely off the road to avoid being hit! I was thankful to have avoided an accident, but I was shaken and found the timing of this incident very suspicious, considering what we were discussing. I ended the conversation with the counselor and hung up, feeling frustrated and disgusted. I was beginning to see just how biblically illiterate and willingly ignorant most "Christians" are regarding demons and spiritual warfare.

Desperate for answers, I began watching anything I could find on television regarding haunting or spiritual warfare, and this led to two very unusual, yet almost identical incidents. One night I found a Christian television program in which evangelist Benny Hinn was teaching about casting out demons. I had the TV on quietly in the bedroom while Chelsea slept. During the program, Benny Hinn explained that once a possessed person comes to a point of repentance, a Christian can command the demon to "Come out in Jesus' name." Immediately when Hinn spoke those words, although Chelsea never awoke, she began squirming in the bed.

A few nights later, I was once again watching TV quietly in bed while Chelsea slept. This time I was watching a program in which a priest was casting a demon out of a boy. During the re-enactment of the exorcism, the priest commanded the demon to

"Come out in Jesus' name." Once again, immediately when those words were spoken, although Chelsea remained sleeping, she began squirming in the bed. I didn't know what to make of those incidents at the time, but it all left me with an unsettled feeling deep inside.

On Saturday, August 26, 2006, as I was getting ready for work, Chelsea violently attacked me again. Considering that I was still healing from a torn pectoral muscle, I suppose she thought I was an easy target. She swung wildly, trying to hit me in the face, but I blocked her punches and again got a hold of her arms and held them down to her sides.

"Stop hitting me!" I told her, but she then began spitting in my face and swearing at me. I remained calm, and eventually she seemed to calm down as well. I had taken several blows, but managed to protect my face. She then calmly walked to the refrigerator and got out a pitcher of Crystal Light and poured herself a glass. Then without warning, she threw the drink into my face and again began punching me! I got my hands up and blocked her punches and restrained her until she calmed down. Her behavior was like Jekyll and Hyde. One moment she was calm, and the next she was like a violent monster!

I then continued trying to get ready for work, but again she charged me, screaming and cussing with fists flailing. Without thinking, and completely by reflex, I grabbed her, spun her around, lifted her off her feet, and threw her to the floor. While screaming more profanities at me, she grabbed the cordless phone and ran to the laundry room. A few moments later, she returned, pretending to suddenly be very loving and apologetic.

"I love you," she said. "Hurry. I don't want you to be late for work."

"You don't even know what love is," I answered as I quickly tried to wash the Crystal Light out of my hair, and then left for work.

*(Years later, after obtaining the police reports from the sheriff's*

department, I learned that Chelsea had made a 911 hang-up call when she briefly left the room and then returned, acting loving and apologetic. Apparently, after dialing the phone, she realized that **she** was the one guilty of assault, and that **she** could be arrested instead of me. Therefore, she shifted gears and acted nice so I'd leave for work, and only she'd be home when the deputy arrived.)

* * *

LATER THAT AFTERNOON, I spoke to a pastor friend I worked with named John, and confided the details of Chelsea's erratic behavior and violent attack that morning.

"Pat, that sounds like demonic possession! For her to be hitting you, spitting in your face, and swearing at you, that sounds like the behavior of someone who is possessed," John insisted. He then prayed with me and promised he'd keep me in his prayers.

One thing is certain, demonic possession or not, for someone to violently attack their spouse in that manner, it is certainly unacceptable and evil behavior with demonic roots. When I returned home that evening after work, Chelsea acted as though nothing had happened and seemed to be her old self, at least temporarily.

Around this same time, I noticed that Chelsea had begun watching A Haunting in the evenings while at home alone. This was completely uncharacteristic, as she now seemed unfazed by the horrific images and storylines. In contrast, while we were dating, she refused to watch horror movies, even with several other couples present. Her behavior also became even ruder and mean-spirited much of the time. Counseling became nothing more than Chelsea verbally abusing me while the counselor sat idly by. During one counseling session, while Chelsea was once again going off on a tirade and attacking my religious beliefs, I'd had enough and walked out.

In September, while Chelsea was away again on a business trip, the atmosphere in the house seemed to become even more ominous. Subtle things would occur as if just to test my sanity. At night, I'd close the curtains only to find them open again after I turned my back. Lights would continue to flicker, and the elusive shadows would occasionally make appearances. I'd also often feel a foreboding presence while praying.

During this time, I tried desperately to find a new church where we could grow spiritually. Sadly, however, with each church we visited, Chelsea would become hostile and argumentative as soon as the sermon ended.

Still hoping for answers, one day I called Chelsea's brother Ed just to see if anyone else in their family had sleep disturbances similar to hers. Ed's answer was not what I was expecting.

"Here's the deal, Pat," he began. "In my first marriage I was cheating on my wife, and I thought I was in love with the other woman. I wanted to look like the good guy, so I treated my wife like crap so *she'd* leave me. That's what Chelsea is doing to you. My advice is to get everything you can. It's sad to say, but I'm closer to you than I am to my own sister."

Ed didn't go into detail about whom Chelsea was cheating with, but he certainly made his point. After hearing this, I began suspecting that possibly she had opened doors to demons in our home by having an affair. Adultery is a very serious sin and certainly has a demonic element to it. I tried in vain to pray and drive the spirits out. I had never cast out a demon or performed an exorcism before, but I did the best I could. I went from room to room and quoted scripture and commanded all demons to leave. I even anointed the doors with oil. Before I finished, I went to our bedroom and anointed the back side of the bedpost on Chelsea's side of the bed.

*(Anointing oil is thought to represent the Holy Spirit and is therefore often used when blessing homes or praying for healing.)*

* * *

I BEGAN STAYING up all night praying, and often I'd have that overwhelming feeling of being watched so heavily that I'd have to keep opening my eyes and looking around to see if someone really *was* there.

One Sunday afternoon, in early October, when Chelsea was about to leave to go to a festival with her mother, I told her that I was going to walk the property, anoint it with oil, and plead the blood of Jesus over everything. Upon hearing this, her demeanor suddenly became aggressive.

*(Pleading the blood of Jesus is an act of faith in which a Christian asks for a covering of the blood of Jesus. Not only does the blood of Jesus wash away our sins in a spiritual sense when we repent, but it also defeated the kingdom of darkness. Therefore the blood of Jesus also protects anything to which it is applied.)*

"You go right ahead, and *you'll* be the one lying on the floor when I get back!" she snarled.

"I don't think so. I've been praying like this over the house already," I answered calmly.

With that, she quickly got into her car and drove off. I found it very peculiar that Chelsea was so hostile to me praying over the property considering she *claimed* to be a Christian and therefore should have welcomed it.

I then walked the entire property and anointed everything with oil and prayed. That night when she returned, she seemed much friendlier. We actually read the Bible together and watched the movie *Flight 93*. By midweek, however, she was back to her old self.

The following Saturday, October 7, when I arrived home from work, she was gone. Strangely enough, it appeared she had left on a whim. There was a Crock-Pot full of food left on, and almost all of her clothes were still hanging in her closet. Several days later, when I finally was able to speak to her on the phone, she made it clear that our marriage was over and she wanted a divorce.

As if that wasn't unsettling enough, she then added in a subdued tone, "Saturday morning at 3:00 a.m., I awoke and heard someone ring the doorbell and then let themself in the house."

"Chelsea, that didn't happen. I was asleep on the couch downstairs, and *I* didn't let anyone in, and I didn't hear *anything*," I answered.

"Well, I heard it," she insisted.

Later, after my head stopped spinning, it occurred to me that Chelsea had never implied that *I* had let someone in, but that someone had rung the doorbell and then let themself in. It was clear that she believed this had happened, considered it paranormal, and wanted no part of it. Considering that I always locked the doors and armed the security system at night, if this did happen, there would be absolutely no explanation.

*Although the foyer was beautiful, it was becoming a location for unexplained activity.*

## CHAPTER SEVEN

### THE DIVORCE

*I* tried to talk sense to Chelsea and told her I didn't want a divorce, but she was ruthless and cunning. I later learned that she was calling our friends and telling them I was crazy. Of course, she made no mention of her repeated violent attacks against me, or her own claims of paranormal activity in the house. She also made no mention of her night terrors, teeth grinding, or strange fear of dolls. No, this was all about ruining my reputation so she would look like the good guy. It was just as her brother Ed had warned.

The remaining months of 2006 were spent negotiating through our attorneys. I was happy to give up our giant-screen Toshiba television in exchange for all the pets. Chelsea put up a fight for Zoe, but I was having none of it. Eventually, I agreed to assume virtually all of the marital debt, and she walked away scot-free. While this might seem like a bad idea, I knew that the property values in eastern Holmes County had skyrocketed after we purchased the land, so I figured there was approximately $100,000 in equity.

Emotionally, I was deeply depressed. I had no friends or family close by, so I felt isolated. When the holidays came, it only got worse. Although in previous years we'd always hosted New Year's Eve parties for all our friends, this year I was alone. I received no phone calls or invitations to others' parties. No one even checked in on me. This only added to the feelings of rejection I was experiencing from Chelsea leaving. The deep bond I already had with my pets was strengthened during this time, however. It was obvious that they were gifts from God.

Strangely enough, the paranormal activity subsided during the months between Chelsea's departure and the divorce, prompting me to suspect the activity *was* linked solely to her.

\* \* \*

WHEN IT CAME time to tell my Amish neighbor Eli and his wife, Anna Mae, that Chelsea had left me and we were divorcing, they weren't at all surprised.

"Well, we knew Chelsea had left you, because Jim Yoder (the mailman) said that she'd gone to the post office to have her mail forwarded to her new address. But we weren't really surprised because we saw cars there a lot too," Anna Mae responded.

"Do you mean you saw cars there a lot while I was at work?" I asked.

"Yes, but we didn't think it was any of *our* business, so we didn't say anything," Anna Mae replied.

After living in Amish country for four years at that point, I had serious doubts that Anna Mae and Eli hadn't said "*anything*" just because they hadn't seen fit to tell *me* what they'd witnessed. I felt quite confident that the subject of Chelsea's company while I was at work had probably been quite the topic of discussion in the Amish community. I also couldn't help but wonder how they'd have felt if Jim had shared *their* personal information that he'd obtained from his job with the United States Postal Service.

*(The fact that Jim had told my personal business, which he was privy to because he was a mailman, proved that he wasn't above*

*breaking the law whenever he saw fit. Considering that he was not only a mailman, but also an elected official as a township trustee, it made me even more suspicious that there was little to no honesty in the Holmes County local government.)*

As it turned out, Eli and Anna Mae weren't the only people to witness strange activity at the house when I wasn't home. A DHL deliveryman made a startling claim one day as well, while I was signing for a package.

"So what do you do for a living that you have to wear that white jacket? Are you a chef?" he asked.

"What white jacket? I don't know what you're talking about," I answered.

"You know, that one day when I made a delivery, you answered the door wearing a white jacket," he replied as if I should remember.

"I'm sorry, sir, but you have the wrong house. That wasn't me," I responded.

"No, I **know** it was this house!" he adamantly proclaimed.

"I assumed the guy in the white jacket was the man of the house, because he signed for the package. I thought it was you," he explained while still looking at me suspiciously, as if he didn't believe me.

I have no idea who the man in the white jacket was, but the DHL driver would have nothing to gain by making up such a strange story. Furthermore, the location of my house made it highly unlikely that he'd have confused my house with another in the area.

I found myself torn between two theories. One was that Chelsea had another man at the house, and he was bold enough to answer the door and sign for our packages. The other theory was that the peculiar man was an apparition. As bizarre as this sounds, I had clearly seen an apparition that looked identical to Zoe, and Chelsea claimed to have seen one that looked exactly like Moses. Furthermore, the man must have looked similar to me because the DHL driver was convinced it *was* me. If a spirit haunting a home can take on the form of pets living there, naturally it could also take on the appearance of the people residing there as well. At that time, I had to err on the side of common sense and conclude that this "door keeper" was in fact someone with whom Chelsea was having extramarital relations.

While pondering this, I remembered another strange incident, which I'd previously downplayed, but now questioned. One night while driving home after work, I called home using my cell phone, and a strange man answered.

"Who's this?" I asked.

"Who's this?" the voice mocked in an arrogant tone. I quickly looked at my phone and confirmed that I had indeed dialed the correct number. I hung up the phone, accelerated my speed, and arrived home just a few minutes later. Upon entering, the house seemed quiet and peaceful, and Chelsea didn't seem the least bit nervous. I convinced myself that the phone lines must have somehow gotten crossed.

These strange stories, coupled with Chelsea's behavior and her brother's claim that she was cheating on me, confirmed that I was divorcing with biblical grounds. Because of my faith, that was important to me, even though a divorce was the last thing I wanted. On February 1, 2007, the divorce was finalized, and I was once again a single man, whether I liked it or not.

CHAPTER EIGHT

EVIL REVEALS ITSELF

*J*t was early February 2007, and for the first time in ten years I would be spending the upcoming Valentine's Day without a significant other. Although the paranormal incidents had tapered off drastically the last few months, now that I was alone and isolated, that wouldn't remain the case. The first incident that occurred after the divorce was so strange and inexplicable that it removed all doubt that the house was haunted.

On Sunday, February 11, I awoke to find that the house felt unusually cold. There had been a substantial amount of snowfall the previous two days, and I was snowed in. I kept the dogs in the garage so I wouldn't have to tread through the deep snow to get to their kennel, which was located at the edge of the backyard, approximately one hundred feet behind the house. Upon feeling how cold the house had become, I quickly checked the thermostats to find the temperature had indeed dropped substantially. Because I had just checked the underground, one-thousand-gallon propane tank the previous week and it was at 40% full, I was baffled.

"Maybe the furnace is broken, or the needle on the gauge of

the propane tank was stuck, and I really am out of fuel," I told myself.

I decided to call my propane supplier and see if they would do an emergency delivery since it was Sunday. I called C&J Gas and explained my predicament to Jeff, who was the owner and manager. After listening patiently, he responded, "I will be happy to do an emergency delivery, but before I drive all the way out there, you should check the vent on your regulator. If your vent is frozen over from the snow, you may not be getting propane through your pipes to the furnace."

I had no idea how to check the vent on the regulator, but Jeff was kind enough to walk me through it. I took my cordless phone and exited the house through the rear patio door. The snow was deep and completely undisturbed as I walked to the side of the house where the regulator was located. I bent over and carefully pushed the deep snow away from the pipe that connected the underground tank to the regulator. As Jeff was explaining how to check the vent, I noticed that the shutoff valve on the pipe was turned off.

"Jeff, the arm on the pipe just below the regulator is turned completely sideways," I interjected.

"Well, that's your shutoff valve. That's your problem. You shut off your valve, so you're not getting any gas to your furnace," Jeff explained. This was bewildering because I knew that as long as I'd lived in the house, I had **never** touched the shutoff valve.

"Could it have been installed wrong?" I asked.

"No, they can't be installed wrong. You must have just turned it off, that's all," he reassured me.

"I never touched it," I answered.

"Well, someone did," Jeff confidently replied.

"Jeff, you don't understand. This snow has been here for two days. Last night I had heat, and this morning I don't. The shutoff valve was under a foot of snow, and the snow was completely undisturbed. How could someone shut off my propane overnight without disturbing the snow or leaving footprints?" I rhetorically asked.

"I can't explain that," Jeff answered and then hesitated before continuing. "But if you turn the valve back on, you should hear the gas go through the line, and if you go back inside and relight your pilot, everything will be fine and you'll have heat again," he added.

I did as Jeff instructed and opened the valve, and just as he said, I heard the gas go through the line. I went back inside to the basement and relit my pilot lights, and the house warmed up again. I was happy to have heat, but disturbed by this latest incident. Without some type of paranormal activity, it was impossible for the shutoff valve to have been closed without the snow being disturbed. Furthermore, if someone had come onto my property and done this, not only would they have disturbed the snow around the regulator, but they'd also have left footprints in the snow.

Another strange incident occurred that same weekend. Because I'd kept Maggie and Copper in the garage due to the weather, I had to take them out every few hours so they could relieve themselves. It was cold and windy as I took Copper out on a leash, and as usual he insisted on walking around a bit before doing his business. Before I knew it, we'd walked all the way down the lane to the road. Maggie was still in her cage inside the garage, and all the doors were shut, so it was impossible for her to see the front yard or driveway. As I was patiently waiting on Copper, I suddenly heard Maggie barking very aggressively. Maggie had a very distinct bark when strangers came around, and this was it! I looked up and saw my Amish neighbor Eli riding his bike on the road, just a few yards away from me. Because of the wind, I hadn't even heard him approaching.

"Boy, Maggie sure is carrying on, isn't she?" he noted as he coasted to a stop.

"Yeah, she is. But what's really strange is that she only barks that way when a stranger comes around, and there's no way she can see or hear you from inside the garage," I answered.

"Yeah, that is strange," Eli agreed as an expression of nervous perplexity chased away his friendly grin. He then quickly pedaled away.

Over the next few weeks, I worked tirelessly to get the house ready to be listed with a Realtor. I just wanted it to sell for the fair market value so I could move on and start a new life. I desperately needed to put the anguish of the last few years behind me. Although the house was beautiful, it represented my destruction. I knew I couldn't keep up the expensive mortgage payments and property taxes indefinitely, and it seemed that everywhere I looked, I was haunted by not only the paranormal, but also sad memories of a failed marriage. Emotionally, I felt as though I was sinking into a deep, dark pit. Spiritually, I was on a roller coaster. I felt oppressed and sometimes found myself questioning and even doubting God. How could He let me suffer like this?

One Sunday evening, while in the living room, I suddenly heard a very loud crash. I looked and saw that the glass cover for the dining room ceiling light had fallen and shattered into hundreds of pieces on the hardwood floor below. I had no explanation for why the cover would suddenly fall. I had changed the bulbs at least three hours earlier that day, and as always, I made sure I had screwed the light cover into place properly. I always double- and triple-checked the light covers when changing the bulbs, because I didn't want a cover to fall and hit my cats or me. There's no way to prove that this incident was paranormal, but I *know* that the light cover had been screwed into place securely. How could it have even stayed in place for over three hours if it hadn't been?

I began watching Christian television almost constantly in hopes that I would learn how to deal with the demonic presence in my home. I stumbled upon a program from Bob Larson, a well-known, controversial exorcist and deliverance minister. I had listened to him on Christian radio many years earlier and knew that he dealt specifically with exorcism, so I ordered some of his videos. Watching these videos not only taught me about spiritual warfare, but also became one of the few ways I was able to sleep at night.

Late one night, while eating my supper in front of the television in the living room, I was reminded once again that I was not alone. As usual, Moses and Zoe had joined me and parked themselves on the floor, to the left of where I sat on the couch. As I was eating, I happened to look towards the tall fireplace that was directly across the room from me. Without warning, I saw in my right peripheral vision what looked like a black shadow of substantial size shoot across the room, passing from the sunroom at the rear of the house and disappearing into the foyer in the front of the house! At the exact same time, in my left periphery, I saw both Moses and Zoe look up and move their heads from right to left, clearly indicating that they'd also witnessed the trajectory of the strange black shadow. This offered proof that my eyes weren't playing tricks on me, and that I truly did see the dark apparition.

I also began noticing strange interference on my telephones. Several times during phone calls to my mother, we'd both hear what sounded like someone else reacting to our conversation. It was almost as if someone else was in my house, listening in on another phone. This was very unsettling.

At that time, I was also becoming increasingly disgruntled with the Church over its rejection of deliverance ministry. It seemed to me that the Church was embracing modern psychology over the Bible. One evening, while discussing this over the phone with Mom, I said, "The church is more concerned with what Carl Jung said than what Jesus Christ said."

As soon as I mentioned the name Carl Jung, there was instantly *very* loud static on the phone. Although I could just barely hear Mom's voice calling out to me, I asked, "Did you notice the static started as soon as I said Carl Jung?" The exact instant I said the name Carl Jung the second time, the static stopped immediately.

*(To those who don't know, Carl Jung is known as the father of modern psychology. Jung claimed to have multiple spirits guiding him, and said that some even possessed him! It is common knowledge that not only was Carl Jung demon possessed, but that he also involved himself with many occult practices, including automatic writing. Sadly, most Christian seminaries educate their students on the teachings of Carl Jung, but little or nothing on Jesus Christ's teachings regarding exorcism and deliverance ministry. This has weakened the Church, and I believe it is why the demons in my house reacted when I mentioned Carl Jung's name.)*

LATE ONE NIGHT, after I had taken the trash out to the edge of the driveway, I found a decorative plate that Chelsea had left inside one of the lower cupboards in the kitchen. The plate showed a painting of the very liberal church that Chelsea had attended while growing up. After Chelsea had gotten saved in the Nazarene Church while we were dating, she told me that the church she grew up in had *never* preached about being born again. Furthermore, after examining the doctrine of that particular denomination, I learned that they embraced ideas that were very much contrary to scripture. I concluded that the doctrines were not merely liberal, but actually demonic.

Remembering this, I considered the plate to be a cursed object and decided I didn't want it in my house. Although it was after 1:00 a.m., I decided to take it out to the trash at the edge of the driveway. I put it in a trash bag and headed to the garage. When I got several feet from the side garage door that I was about to exit, I suddenly felt a strong burst of air hit me in the face! With no doors or windows open in the garage, there was absolutely no explanation for this. Needless to say, I had an eerie feeling as I walked to the end of the dark lane and back to the house, but there was no way I wanted that plate in my house another day.

These strange occurrences were forcing me to study my Bible even more, in search of information about spiritual warfare and casting out demons. I was amazed at how little the Church was teaching about a subject in which the Bible contained such a vast wealth of knowledge. Jesus spoke of binding demons (Matthew 12:28–29; Mark 3:27) and casting them out, and he made it clear that I, along with all born-again Christians, have the authority to do this (Mark 16:17). Not knowing what else to do, I often prayed and, in Jesus' name, bound whatever demons were in the house. I commanded the demons to leave many times, but to no avail. I figured if they weren't leaving, perhaps I could at least limit their power by binding them.

*(Sadly the practice of binding demons is usually ignored or scoffed at in the church today. After practicing the binding of demons for many years now, I can attest that when a Christian binds demons in Jesus' name, something powerful happens in the spiritual realm that effectively incapacitates the demon's power. Situations truly can change suddenly when Christians stand in their God-given authority and bind the enemy!)*

.

# CHAPTER NINE

## HOUSE FOR SALE

*I*n late winter/early spring, I had the property surveyed and broken into two plots, with the front two acres and the house separated from the rear four acres. On March 27, 2007, I listed the property with a Realtor and hoped for the best. I didn't know it at the time, but my problems would soon get much worse. Putting the house up for sale was a sad reminder of all that I'd lost the previous five years, and I knew if it didn't sell quickly, I could lose everything.

With the house and land now on the market, I was concerned that it might be a hard sell, considering that the trustees had still not paved the road. While the house was being built, five years earlier, Jonus had assured me that his cousin Jim and the other township trustees would pave the road once the house was completed. After my disputes with Jonus, however, I was convinced that Jim was holding a grudge. Not only were the trustees not paving the road, but once the Realtor sign went up in the yard, they stopped putting gravel on the road too. The dusty road now had multiple potholes, making the sale of my house virtually impossible. Several times I saw Amish people pulling up in their buggies and taking all of the Realtor flyers so there wouldn't be any left for potential buyers. Once, I even saw Jim taking flyers after putting my mail in the mailbox. My frustration was growing every day.

On April 24, around 4:30 p.m., I was working in the yard when I looked up and couldn't believe what I saw. Isaac was once again trespassing on my land. He crossed my land in his buggy to get to his landlocked parcel behind my property. My patience with him had worn thin, so I called the sheriff. Isaac would have to come back across my property to get back home, and I hoped the deputy would be there by that time so he could witness it. Before the deputy arrived, Isaac attempted to cross my property again, but I stopped him.

"Isaac, stop your buggy and wait right there. I called the sheriff, and they're on their way. You're trespassing *again*, and I've had enough," I told him.

"Do I trespass on your land, Isaac?" I asked.

"Well, no," he responded.

"Haven't I warned you before to stop trespassing?"

"Yes," he answered nonchalantly.

During the next few minutes, while I waited for the deputy to arrive, I voiced my opinion about the hypocrisy I'd witnessed from the Amish. I'm not implying that this was the right thing to do, but I'd tried to be patient with Isaac for years, and now my patience had run out.

"So let me get this straight, Isaac. You're forbidden to drive a car, have a phone in your house, or wear deodorant, but you're allowed to cuss, steal, smoke, drink alcohol, abuse your horses, molest your children, and trespass on your neighbor's land? What kind of religion is that?" I asked.

"Yes, but I don't molest my children," he answered while purposely ignoring the other issues I'd raised.

The deputy finally arrived, and I explained how I'd had multiple incidents with Isaac and his family trespassing, and that I'd warned him repeatedly to stop.

"Is that true, Mr. Raber?" the deputy asked.

"I don't remember," Isaac answered. With that lie, I became livid.

"What do you mean you don't remember? You just acknowledged a few minutes before the deputy arrived that I've warned you to stop trespassing. Don't even sit there and play dumb now!" I snapped.

"Now you wait a minute! I'm not going to let you talk to Mr. Raber like that," the deputy scolded.

"Don't *you* tell *me* how to talk to anyone," I fired back at the deputy. "You wouldn't even be here if I hadn't called you! My taxes pay your salary. Your job is to protect and serve. He's trespassing on my land right now in front of you!"

The deputy then explained very gingerly to Isaac that if I'd warned him to stop trespassing, then he was breaking the law if he continued to do so.

"Do you want to file charges on him?" the deputy asked as he turned to me.

Although I was very incensed, I thought for a minute before answering. "No, I'll let it slide this time." I then directed my attention back to Isaac.

"I'm not filing charges against you, but I want you and the other Amish to leave me alone! Stop trespassing on my land, and stop bothering me! If you all hate me so much, buy my house and I'll move away!"

As the deputy and Isaac left, I hoped that my act of mercy would show the Amish that I wasn't the bad guy, and maybe they'd finally treat me with respect. Shortly thereafter, my Realtor informed me that several Amish people had called and inquired about my house and land. When he told them my asking price, the one Amish lady snapped back, "Well, I want it, but I'm not paying that!"

On May 28 as I was again working in my yard, I saw several individuals on four-wheelers a short distance from the house, and they were doing donuts in the road. I was infuriated because the road was already in terrible condition, and they were making it much worse. I went inside and called the sheriff and explained the situation to the dispatcher, who then placed me on hold. As I waited, the individuals on the four-wheelers continued tearing up the road, so I hung up the phone and decided to talk to them myself.

I approached them and told them to stop immediately. As I was explaining to them that they were breaking the law and I wouldn't tolerate it, one of them ran to a nearby house and called the sheriff and reported that I'd made death threats. This claim was completely false, and when the deputy and state patrol arrived, I explained that I had not threatened anyone's life. I then showed them the large round ruts in the road. They refused to issue citations to anyone, but warned me about making threats. Once again I requested more patrols in Eastern Holmes County, but my request fell on deaf ears.

# CHAPTER TEN

## MY FIRST EXORCISM

*A*fter listing the house with a Realtor, I decided to try having some open houses to hopefully attract potential buyers. One Saturday, a few friends and relatives came to help me prepare for the open house the next day. One such individual was an old family friend named Danielle. Danielle and her husband, Jeff, had been close to our family for many years and seemed more like extended family than friends. Strangely enough, Danielle had undergone an exorcism a few weeks earlier with an exorcist named Pastor Tom from Youngstown, Ohio. For several months prior to that exorcism, Danielle and I'd had several conversations about spiritual warfare. As I had explained to her what I was dealing with in my house, and what I was learning about demons, she became convinced that she might actually be a victim of possession. She traveled to Youngstown and met with Pastor Tom, who'd been trained by Bob Larson. Her fears proved to be true. She manifested demons, and several were cast out. Although the exorcism was successful, she believed there were still some unresolved issues and further deliverance might be necessary.

Late in the afternoon that Saturday, I was working on the

staircase when I saw Danielle standing below in the foyer, looking up at me with a puzzled expression on her face.

"What?" I asked. She didn't answer but instead just shook her head and walked away into the dining room. Later, Danielle once again approached me.

"When I was in the foyer and you were on the stairs, did you call my name?" she asked.

"No. I didn't say anything. I just noticed you looking at me weird, so I asked what you wanted," I answered.

"I'm sure I heard a man's voice call my name. I assumed it was you because no one else was around," she insisted. Danielle was obviously troubled by the incident, but we all kept working.

The open house the following day didn't generate any interest in the house, so my frustration deepened. I tried to dig my heels in and trust God, but the depression from the divorce seemed to haunt me every waking hour, and the loneliness of the secluded house only fueled the fire.

The week after the open house, my mother informed me that she had been in contact with Danielle and that her behavior seemed very odd and almost erratic. Mom said that Danielle had made an appointment with Pastor Tom for another exorcism, but it wouldn't be for a few weeks.

One night very late, I was feeling desperate, so I decided to email some prayer requests to Bob Larson's ministry. I went to my home office, logged on to my computer, and began typing. At first, I was only requesting prayer for my situation regarding the strange activity in my house, and my need for a quick sale. I then began requesting prayer for Danielle, and informed Mr. Larson that she had undergone one exorcism with Pastor Tom, and was going to be going through another. As I then began to relate the story involving Danielle hearing a man's voice call her name in my foyer, I suddenly felt a very evil presence enter the office. The hair on the back of my neck stood up, and I got intense goose-bumps. I slowly turned around and looked over my left shoulder, fully expecting to see a sinister entity standing there. Nothing was visible, but the evil I felt was overwhelming. I slowly turned and looked at a painting of *The Last Supper*, which was hanging on the wall to my right. When I looked into Jesus' eyes in the picture, I felt confirmation in my spirit that I was not alone in the office, and that there was indeed an evil spirit present. It's difficult to fully explain spiritual discernment. Although I didn't see anything, I *knew* something evil was there and making its presence felt.

I slowly stood up and struggled to the office door. I had difficulty walking because it felt as though an unseen hand was pressing against my chest, and my legs felt like they each weighed a ton! It was almost as if I were struggling against a strong, unseen current of water. I was completely terrorized as I made my way out of the office, through the foyer, and to the telephone in the dining room. I grabbed the receiver, hoping to call Mom for prayer. When I put the phone to my ear, I realized that my dial-up internet was still connected, and I'd have to go back into the office and log off before making the call! Terrified or not, I had no choice. I forced myself to go back into the office and logged off the internet. I then called Mom, and after we prayed together, the creepy feeling seemed to dissipate.

As we continued talking, I noted that it was abundantly obvious that whatever was in the house didn't want me to tell Bob Larson about the strange voice Danielle had heard calling her name in my foyer! Before we ended our conversation, I shared a strange hunch I'd been having.

"I can't tell you how I know this, but I know the name of a demon Danielle has, and I also know the number six is significant!"

The following Monday evening I received a call from Danielle, who was with Mom, and needed to ask a favor of me.

"When I go to see Pastor Tom again, will you go with me?"

"Sure, I'll go with you, but I know what you've got, and I'm spilling the beans to Pastor Tom," I calmly answered. After a few moments of dead silence, Danielle replied, "Don't say anything else."

Somehow, at that moment I knew that her demons were about to manifest, and she was trying to keep them down. She handed the phone to Mom and went to the next room while we chatted. The next thing I knew, Danielle began freaking out. I could hear a strange voice in the background.

"Get down here right away, Patrick. We need your help!" Mom pleaded as she hung up the phone.

I grabbed my Bible and headed for my car. As I was driving, I noticed that the hair on my arms was standing straight up. Unlike the recent incident in my home office, however, this time the feeling I had was *not* fear! Although I'd never performed an exorcism before, I felt confident and empowered by the Holy Spirit! When I arrived, I rushed in through the garage and found Danielle sitting in a chair while Mom held a Bible against her. Danielle's face was contorted, and a strange voice was coming out of her.

"Tell me your name!" Mom commanded.

The demon shrieked and snarled, but refused to answer. Upon seeing this and without a second thought, I interrupted, "I know who you are, Jezebel, and you're leaving today!"

"How did you know?" the demon screamed.

"God told me!" I boldly proclaimed.

Over the next several hours, I, with help from Mom, my sister Lory, and brother-in-law Matt, systematically drove eight demon spirits out of Danielle. It turned out that the number six was indeed significant. The Jezebel spirit had possessed Danielle because of a generational curse from an ancestor who practiced witchcraft six generations earlier. I was now beginning to under-stand that I had a gift of discernment, because there was no way for me to have known the Jezebel spirit's name or that the number six was significant. Between Pastor Tom and I, Danielle was making progress, but I suspected her deliverance was still not complete.

Later, as I returned home, it was clear to me that God was using my terrible situation for the good of others. Because of my predicament, I was learning biblical truths that I had never heard in Church. These truths were crucial in helping others become free from demonic bondage. I couldn't help but wonder, however, why I seemed to still be trapped in a living hell. How could I cast demons out of a person, but not be able to rid my own house of their presence? How could I discern what demons another person had, yet not be able to discern the elusive secret that kept me enslaved? The irony of it all seemed like a cruel joke. I felt very uneasy that night upon returning home, and I slept with an open Bible on my chest.

# CHAPTER ELEVEN

## OPPRESSED

hroughout the remainder of 2007, I was tormented by both the paranormal occurrences and more provocation from my neighbors. Hoping for some clue that might deliver me from this nightmare, I continued watching television shows about the paranormal, as well as Christian programs. Although I didn't believe in ghosts, watching *Ghost Hunters* gave me peace of mind that I wasn't crazy, and that houses can indeed be haunted. One Wednesday evening, I was watching *Ghost Hunters* as I did work around the house. During a commercial break, I was in the laundry room and clearly saw Zoe enter just as I was about to exit. When I entered the living room, I looked across the open dining room into the kitchen and saw Zoe perched on top of the cupboard! I immediately went back into the laundry room and found it empty. Moses was nowhere around either. This was very similar to an experience I'd had years earlier, and once again there was no explanation.

I also began noticing strange aromas in the house late at night. At times I'd inexplicably smell cigarette smoke. Then one evening, as I was standing in the kitchen, I began smelling the distinct smell of an old perfume from Avon called "Sweet

Honesty." I hadn't smelled it in many years, but my mom wore it when I was a child, and there was no mistaking the smell. Just as in the case of the elusive cigarette smell, I was unable to find any source for this aroma.

One night, I was in the home office, drinking a cup of coffee as I surfed the internet. I finished my coffee and set the mug on a coaster that was on the desk just to my left. A short while later, inexplicably, I heard the spoon that I'd used to stir in creamer and had left in the mug suddenly move by itself! It was as if some unseen hand had pulled the spoon away from the inside of the mug and then let go so it would fall, making a loud noise. I tried in vain to re-enact the incident and find a natural explanation, but the spoon had clearly moved by itself!

I would also frequently notice Maggie looking in one direction and barking very aggressively, as if she saw something that upset her, but I could see nothing. Late one night, when I went out to feed and water Maggie and Copper, somehow my home security system became armed. When I opened the side garage door, the alarm went off. I know I didn't set the alarm before going outside, and only I had the security code, which was necessary to arm or disarm the alarm. I could find no explanation for how this could have happened. Strangely enough, although I lived alone, seemingly in the middle of nowhere, I'd often go outside to the kennel to check on the dogs at all hours of the night. Sometimes I even did this at three or four o'clock in the morning, but it wasn't like I had good sleeping patterns anymore. I also began noticing that when I happened to be outside between 3:00 and 4:00 a.m., I'd hear a strange noise coming from Isaac Raber's farm. It was somewhat like the sound of someone holding a piece of metal to a grinding wheel. The sound was very loud and would last for several seconds.

I was also beginning to realize that in a haunted house, aside from the paranormal experiences, the demonic oppression is daunting. The feelings of hopelessness and despair were overwhelming. I came to understand that this is because demon spirits have no hope of redemption, and therefore they impose their hopelessness on their victims. Because of these negative feelings, at times I doubted and rebelled against God because I couldn't understand why He was allowing me to suffer so grievously if He loved me. There were days I completely gave up and vowed I wouldn't follow Jesus any longer, but then like the Apostle Peter, I found myself coming to the realization that Jesus holds the words of eternal life, and there was nowhere else to turn but to Him (John 6:68). Trying to live without Him wasn't really living at all. Looking back now, I am truly thankful that His mercies are new each morning (Lamentations 3:23). I can also truthfully say that each time I sank to those depths, God sent a message through scripture, a Christian friend, or a speaker on Christian television to remind me that I *had* to keep fighting. Giving up was not an option.

One morning, while the depression had me almost completely hopeless, I cried out to God to just take my life. I knew the demons around me wanted me to commit suicide, but I fought back. I knew that no matter how bad my life seemed, it was still better than being in Hell for eternity. I was so weary from my fight that I not only asked God to just take me out, but I also questioned why he'd let me be born just to suffer this type of oppression. At that time, He seemed to remain silent.

Later that day, I opened my Bible right to the book of Job, chapters 3 and 4. At the top of one page it read "Job Curses His Birth," and at the top of the next page it read "Job Longs for Death." When I read those words, I was instantly reminded that even Job had experienced the *exact* same negative emotions while under demonic attack. I was also reminded that in the end, Job was victorious. With that, I mustered up the strength to pick myself up and fight another day.

Over that summer the Amish annoyances progressed. They were still stealing the Realtor flyers, and some would even make appointments to view the house, only to make ridiculously low offers just to get under my skin. One Saturday morning at a gas station, several young Mennonite and Amish men started an argument with me. It certainly was not the Christian thing to do, but I let my anger get the best of me. While they were cussing at me from their work truck, I approached them and called them out. Although I was livid, I kept my composure. Again, I was outnumbered, but I had no fear, and I'm ashamed to admit it, but I wanted to hurt them.

"Wow, that's really scary. You know how to cuss! Now if you really think you're tough, get out of the truck," I said in a quiet even tone. I could feel myself giving over to the rage that was brewing inside me. They continued cussing but remained in the truck.

"Look, I have somewhere I need to be. I don't have all day. If you want to fight, get out of the truck. It won't take long, and then I can go to work, and you all can go to the hospital," I added. They refused to get out but kept hurling profanities.

"That's real nice language," I said as I headed back to my vehicle and drove off.

I was ashamed of the way I handled the situation and the deep anger I felt towards those men, but the pressure I was under was taking its toll. Once again, I had to pray and ask forgiveness.

After this incident, several times when I'd return home from work, I noticed Amish buggy wheel marks in my yard and piles of horse droppings. There were multiple wheel prints, and it was easy to see that more than one buggy had driven through the yard. Apparently the Amish thought this was funny, but I wasn't amused. I was seeing firsthand that their religious veneer was a lie.

# CHAPTER TWELVE

## IRISH 19

One August Sunday afternoon, as I wallowed in hopelessness and despair, I received an urgent phone call from Mom.

"Danielle is here, and we need your help! This morning in church she started manifesting demons, so Jeff brought her here because they feared no one at church would know how to deal with this. Please get down here right away!" Mom pleaded. (Danielle had undergone several exorcisms already and had made progress each time, but we all knew she had not yet received complete deliverance.)

"I'm in no condition right now to cast out anything! My faith is weak, and if I come down there, the demons are going to kick my teeth out! They're setting me up!" I argued from my haze of oppression and self-pity.

I could hear strange noises in the background and that familiar demonic snarl in Danielle's voice. Mom put the phone down and told Jeff what I'd said. A few minutes later Mom returned to the phone.

"Jeff said to tell you that your faith is stronger than you think because those demons do **not** want you here!"

How could I argue with that? I explained that I was going to pray and I'd be there as soon as possible. In my depression, I hadn't eaten since the previous day, so *technically* I had fasted. I lay facedown on the floor and spent some time in prayer, pouring my heart out to God. I asked for His forgiveness for my faithlessness and rebellion. I also asked for the empowering of the Holy Spirit as well. I prayed until I felt God's peace come over me, and then I hit the road, ready for another showdown with demon spirits.

Mom lived three counties away, so I had more time to pray and prepare while I drove. When I arrived, I already knew exactly what type of demon I'd encounter because God had shown me this through discernment. I quietly entered the house, and although Danielle had no idea I was there, her demons immediately manifested, as if on cue. The entire exorcism took many hours and was extremely intense and dramatic, but when the smoke cleared, nineteen demons had been driven out in Jesus' mighty name.

From what I could tell, Danielle's possession was rooted in several generational curses from her Irish ancestry. As I headed back home, I thanked God for His mercy and grace, as I felt even more strongly that He had a call on my life for deliverance ministry. I couldn't understand, however, why I could help others get free from their demons, yet I felt completely trapped in my own satanic nightmare.

One evening a few weeks later, as I returned home from work, I had yet another reminder of how vast the network of demons possessing my house really was. As always, I'd locked all the doors and armed the security system, so when I arrived, I unlocked the door and disarmed the alarm before heading to the office to check my email. I turned on the computer and went to my home page, but when I attempted to log in to my email, I saw that in the username box, something was already typed. It read "IRISH19."

"How can that be?" I asked myself. Was someone trying to hack my email? But then I realized that even if someone tried to hack my email, the username they typed in wouldn't show up on my computer unless they were attempting to hack the account *from* my computer! Considering my doors were all locked and the security system was armed while I was away, it was impossible that someone could have entered the house without setting off the alarm. The spirits in the house had manipulated my computer!

"But what could IRISH19 mean?" I asked myself. Then I realized that it was a reference to the nineteen demons I'd cast out of Danielle several weeks earlier, on that Sunday afternoon in August. The demons in my house were taunting me and attempting to inflict fear by implying that those nineteen demons were now visiting me. The incident made me angry rather than scared, and I again prayed and bound the demons in Jesus' name. Nevertheless, I couldn't help but wonder when it all would end.

# CHAPTER THIRTEEN

## TORMENTED

*I*n October, I decided to speak to one of the township trustees other than Jim Yoder, in an attempt to get my road paved. I contacted a trustee named Jon Mast and explained my situation of trying to sell the house while the road remained in such bad condition. Jon treated me with respect, so I decided to tell him about my suspicions that Jim was holding a grudge against me.

"I believe Jim is singling me out because he doesn't like me. Other roads have been paved, and I deserve to have mine paved as well," I explained.

"You're right, Jim doesn't like you at all. I don't know why, but he has brought your name up many times in our meetings, and he definitely has a problem with you," Jon agreed.

"Well, I'm a taxpaying citizen, and Jim's an elected official, so if he's treating me any differently than other citizens, it's discrimination," I reminded Jon before the call ended.

Now my frustration only deepened. Jim really was punishing me for standing up to his rotten cousin Jonus. I was sure that discrimination from an elected official was illegal, but what could

I really do about it? It was painfully obvious that Holmes County was a great example of small-town politics at its worst.

On November 6, I noticed that someone had damaged my Realtor sign, and there was a substantial hole right through the middle of it. Again I called the sheriff, filed another complaint, and requested more patrols in my area. As usual, my request was ignored. I was sure it was the Amish who'd damaged the sign, but without seeing it firsthand, there was nothing I could do. To be honest, I wasn't so sure the sheriff's department would do anything even if I had seen who'd done it.

A few weeks later, I received a call from a man who expressed interest in the house. The man's last name sounded very foreign, and I suspected he was Indian. Remembering a rumor I'd heard about the Amish being racist, I decided to tell my neighbor Eli about it and watch his reaction. A few days later, when I went to my mailbox to get my mail, I saw him riding by on his bike.

"Hey, Eli, I've got some good news," I told him as he stopped his bike.

"What's that?" he asked.

"I just spoke to a guy who sounded interested in the house! You may have new neighbors before you know it, and I think they're Indians from India! Isn't that great?"

"Oh, really? Hmmm," Eli said as the smile left his face. He suddenly seemed irritated and said he had to get home, and he quickly pedaled away. A short while later, I saw Eli pass my house, looking very frantic as his horse galloped in front of his buggy. I watched as Eli then made his way down the road and up the long lane to his father's house, which overlooked the valley.

Much later that evening, long after dark, I was standing at my kitchen sink, about to drink a glass of water. As I raised the glass to my mouth, my eyes fell upon my reflection in the window behind the sink, and I clearly saw a black shadow behind me, as if it was looking over my left shoulder. Just as I saw it, the shadow quickly disappeared in a downward motion. The overhead lighting was above and slightly behind me, so there wasn't even a remote possibility that the shadow could have been mine. The fact that it disappeared in a downward motion was even more eerie!

The following night, when I returned home from work at approximately 10:40 p.m., everything seemed peaceful and quiet. Later, however, between 1:00 and 2:00 a.m., I heard a strange loud noise. The next morning, I found that my Realtor sign and the dispenser for the real estate flyers had been smashed to pieces and scattered all over the ground. Once again, I called the sheriff and reported the vandalism, and when the deputy arrived, I shared my suspicion that Eli had either done this or knew who did. The deputy didn't seem all that interested in getting to the bottom of it, but he did agree to talk to Eli. Of course, Eli claimed to know nothing, but after the deputy finished questioning him, his wife left me a voicemail stating that their cows had gotten out just *before* dark on the night in question, and that she was sorry if the cows caused any damage.

Considering that I had gotten home at 10:40 p.m., which was long *after* dark, and the sign and dispenser had been undamaged at that time, I knew she was lying and found it almost comical that they blamed the vandalism on their poor cows. It was obvious to me that this latest incident was an act of retaliation against me because Eli didn't want *Indian* neighbors. I suspected that the dark shadow I'd witnessed the previous night was related to this incident as well, but I was still unsure how all the pieces fit together.

In December, I had more incidents with the Amish trespassing and harassing me with phone calls. Each incident was reported to the sheriff's department, but it was abundantly clear that they had no intention of enforcing the law. After one harassing phone call in which I was cussed out for reporting trespassing, I told the deputy that I wanted him to file charges. Later, when I obtained all the police reports, I found that the deputy had noted that I wanted to file charges, yet he neglected to follow through. It appeared that in Holmes County "Protect and Serve" was only a slogan.

My calls to the sheriff's department were *rewarded*, however, when I was then selected for jury duty. I was selected as juror #1, and to this day, I still believe this nuisance was a subtle punishment for my repeated complaints to the sheriff's department about the Amish. I called the court and explained that in my line of work, I often had to testify in court on behalf of the prosecution.

"It's going to be very difficult to be open minded because in my line of work, I'm always on the side of the prosecution," I explained.

"You're not getting out of this!" the bailiff fired back.

When the day of the trial arrived, I reported for jury duty with a doctor's excuse in hand. Although I saw many potential jurors relieved from duty for much pettier reasons, the courts refused to excuse me. I followed through with my service and was selected by the other jurors as the foreman. After witnessing the inside workings of the court system during that trial, I believed more than ever that there was no real justice in Holmes County.

# CHAPTER FOURTEEN

## 911

*A*s 2008 began, it was obvious that the oppression I was experiencing showed no signs of letting up. On January 10, in the very early morning hours, I had a very strange nightmare in which I was performing an exorcism on a man I'd never seen before. The man's name was Kenny, and he had long gray hair and was very odd looking. Just as Kenny's demons began manifesting, the dream suddenly ended. Later, at approximately 7:45 a.m., I was awakened by the sound of my phone ringing. I was very groggy as I put the receiver to my ear.

"Hello," I said.

"This is the Holmes County Sheriff's Department. Are you alright?" a voice on the other end of the line asked.

"Yes, I'm alright. Why would you call me at 7:50 in the morning and ask if I'm ok?" I asked as I rubbed my eyes and looked at my alarm clock, which I always set slightly fast.

"Because you just called 911 and hung up," the dispatcher answered.

"No, I didn't!" I replied as that familiar creepy feeling came over me.

"Yes, you did!"

"Look, I didn't call you! I was sleeping, and *you* woke *me* up!"

"Well, if you didn't call, then someone else in your house did."

"You don't understand. I live alone. It's just me and my cats, and I didn't call you."

"Well, a deputy is on his way," the dispatcher informed me before hanging up.

I immediately went throughout the entire house, looking everywhere to make sure someone wasn't hiding. My doors and windows were all locked, and the security system was still armed. I even looked in every closet. I was totally alone, and considering the phone call coincided with my strange demonic nightmare, I was sure they were related. When the deputy arrived, I explained the situation and assured him that I didn't make the phone call.

"You can think I'm crazy if you want, but I'm telling you the truth. Weird things go on out here! I have creepy things happen all the time that I can't explain," I asserted. The deputy didn't even bat an eye, and somehow I knew he believed me.

One night a few weeks later, as I got ready for bed, I decided to watch a DVD of one of my favorite evangelists, John Bevere. When the house was built, I'd had every room wired so whatever was being watched on the television in the living room downstairs could be seen on any TV in any room upstairs. I put the DVD in the player in the living room and pressed play. I then turned the living room TV off and laid the remote control on the coffee table, facing away from the TV. As always, I then double-checked the security alarm, made sure the doors were locked, and shut off the lights before going upstairs to my bedroom.

I then went to bed, set the timer on my TV to shut off in one hour, and fell asleep listening to John Bevere's sermon. The next morning when I awoke, although my bedroom TV was off, I could hear a strange loud noise. I got up and went downstairs to find that the living room TV had been turned back on, and loud static was coming from the speaker. I turned the TV off and looked at the coffee table, and just as I remembered, the remote control was still facing *away* from the TV, exactly as I had left it. Even if the remote *had* been facing the TV, it would have been impossible to turn the TV on because the oak coffee table had sides that stuck up approximately one inch higher than the table's top and blocked the signal. I left the remote control flat on the table but turned it towards the TV and tried to turn the TV on. All attempts were unsuccessful. I believe that these types of paranormal activity were being done as a reminder that the entities were still present despite my attempts to cast them out. The doom and gloom I constantly felt was more than a reminder, but these incidents invoked more fear, anger and frustration.

# CHAPTER FIFTEEN

## MORE PROVOCATION

On February 3, when I returned home from work, I noticed that someone had driven either a four-wheeler or small car or truck through my yard, leaving ruts. Again, I called the sheriff and filed a complaint and requested more patrols in my area. Then on February 13, I returned home from work to discover that someone had driven a snowmobile deep into my yard and left a large path before returning back to the road. It was clear that someone was just trying to annoy me. I decided to follow the tracks through the snow and found that they led right into a barn on an Amish farm about a mile from my house. *Again,* I called the sheriff, and when the deputy arrived, I explained what happened, showed him the tracks, and told him that I wanted to file charges.

"Well, there's no way to know who did this," he claimed.

"Really? I followed the tracks to the farm about a mile down the road, and the snowmobile is in the barn," I explained. Sensing he was going to do nothing, I then added, "Either *you* can do something, or *I* will!"

Because I forced their hand, the sheriff's department did an investigation and identified who had driven the snowmobile through my yard. They then concluded, however, that the suspect was really sorry, so they didn't want to file charges. Ultimately, nothing was done, and it was once again clear that the Amish in Holmes County make their own laws. Because I stirred the pot by forcing the sheriff's department to investigate, the Amish unleashed yet another attack of harassment against me.

The next Sunday afternoon, I received a call from an Amish man named Jacob Troyer. I didn't take the call, so Jacob left a message on the answering machine, saying he was interested in buying my entire property.

"Yeah, right! Amish don't do business on Sundays! This is another setup," I told myself after listening to his message.

It was clear to me that this was another prank designed to get my hopes up, only to dash them. I ignored the message and didn't return his call. A couple of days later, my Realtor Mike Smith called me and said that Jacob had called him and was really interested in purchasing my entire property.

"Mike, I'm sorry, but I know better than that. Since when do the Amish conduct business on Sunday afternoon? My guess is that they sat in their church and concocted a plan to get under my skin, and then went right home and called me. They aren't serious, and I'm not wasting my time," I explained.

"He's saying he's interested, Pat. You have to call him back," Mike insisted.

"Ok, I'll do it, but I guarantee he's not serious, and they're just messing with me *again*," I assured him.

Mike gave me Jacob's cell phone number, and I called him. Jacob seemed overjoyed at the prospect of buying the entire property and house, and claimed he definitely wanted it. He said he was just waiting for his bank to approve him, which he assured me would be no problem. A few more weeks went by, and Jacob kept in contact with me, always insisting that he would have no problem getting the money to buy my property. Then the phone calls stopped. Eventually, I contacted Jacob again, and what he told me proved that my first hunch was correct.

"Yeah, hey, it turns out that I got an offer to lease to buy a property from Holmes Limestone, and there's a three-story house on forty-two acres, and it's only $250 per month, and it's all land contract," Jacob claimed in an upbeat tone as if I was supposed to believe such a preposterous story.

I knew he was lying but decided to call Holmes Limestone and verify his claim. When I spoke to them, they assured me that they had no such property and that they'd never spoken with Jacob Troyer and didn't even know who he was.

Frustrated, I called an old friend of mine named Jerry Mullet, who was of Mennonite heritage and had keen insight into the Amish and Mennonite communities. Jerry had also worked in law enforcement in Holmes County for many years and believed the current sheriff to be corrupt and "on the take" with the Amish. I explained what I was going through, and Jerry offered some advice.

"Pat, first off, tell this Amish fella you're going to the bishop of his church if he doesn't stop harassing you. If that doesn't work, tell him you're calling the news media. The Amish don't like for people to find out what *really* goes on behind the scenes, so tell him that he'll be on TV if he keeps it up."

Before ending our call, Jerry assured me that both the sheriff and court system in Holmes County cater to the Amish.

"The Amish get elected whomever *they* want elected. Then, as long as these people do what the Amish want, they'll keep their jobs. If they start going against the Amish, the Amish will back someone else in the next election. This sheriff is corrupt," Jerry said.

The next day I called Jacob and tested Jerry's advice.

"Jacob, I'm curious. Who's your bishop?" I asked.

"My dad, Jacob Troyer Senior," he replied. Knowing that telling his bishop was no longer a viable option, I shifted gears.

"Have you ever been on TV before, buddy?" I asked in a friendly tone.

"No. Can't say I have," he replied as his voice cracked.

"Well, if you mess with me again, you will be! I know you were never interested in my house or property and were just harassing me. If you harass me again, I'm calling the news channels out of Cleveland and letting them know what the Amish *really* are!" I warned.

Jacob backed down, and I never heard from him again. The Amish harassment greatly subsided for a while after that, but the paranormal activity increased. Although I'd seen through the recent harassment from the start, it still accomplished its goal. I was sure from the beginning that Jacob was lying, but there had been a small flicker of hope that he really was interested in the property. When that flicker was snuffed out, my anger, frustration and hopelessness grew.

Late one night when I was at my worst, I decided to take matters into my own hands. I was frustrated and angry from the harassment, so I concocted a plan to be a nuisance to my Amish neighbors to see how they liked it. Right then, the Holy Spirit checked me. I thought for a minute that what I was about to do was wrong, but because I was so fed up, I decided to do it anyway.

At that very moment, the light in the room began flickering wildly. Recognizing that this was a demon reacting to my decision for revenge, I immediately repented. "God forgive me," I said out loud as fear gripped me. As soon as those words left my mouth, the lights stopped flickering and returned to normal! Although my neighbors' behavior was evil, it was not my place to pay them back. Vengeance belongs to God (Romans 12:19).

# CHAPTER SIXTEEN

## PROVOKED BY PRAYER

$\mathcal{I}$ was completely isolated in my struggle. It seemed my friends were nowhere to be found, so I often unloaded my emotional baggage on my mom. One night around 2:40 a.m., she awoke very worried about me. She continually prayed for me, but this time she felt she needed to ask others to pray as well. She called a twenty-four-hour prayer line and explained my situation to a prayer counselor. This counselor then prayed with Mom and lifted all my needs to God. When the prayer was over and Mom hung up the phone, she felt relieved.

"That was a powerful prayer," she thought to herself. Just then, she heard three very loud knocks on her door! She looked at the clock, and it was exactly 3:00 a.m.! She got up and went to the door, but no one was there, and outside there was dead silence. Mom instantly recognized that some evil spirit was angry because she'd called the prayer line.

There are two more interesting elements to the incident. First, the fact that it occurred between 3:00 and 4:00 a.m. is significant because this is known as the "witching hour" or the "devil's hour." This is because 3:00 a.m. is the time Jesus Christ was crucified, according to Jewish methods of timekeeping.

Currently, we use a method similar to the methods of time-keeping that the Romans used, which would have been more likely around 9:00 a.m., but Jesus was Jewish. Demons combine these two methods to bring confusion. Ironically, demons also know that in reality, Jesus defeated Satan when he laid down his life, so they want to distract from the truth. Therefore, demonic paranormal activity often occurs during this hour of the day to mock the crucifixion. Secondly, there were *three* very loud knocks at the door. Demonic spirits often do things in threes to mock the Trinity.

Later when Mom related the story to me, she said, "It really didn't sound like someone *knocking* on the door, it sounded like someone was trying to *knock the door down!*"

Considering that Mom lived three counties away from me, it was obvious that whatever I was up against was powerful. I believe that in the most extreme haunts, demons will attack those trying to help, even if they are geographically far removed from the haunted location. I couldn't help but wonder if some greater evil might have befallen me if she hadn't prayed.

# CHAPTER SEVENTEEN

CALL MY NAME

*O*n Wednesday evening, April 23, 2008, as I was driving home from work, the deep depression once again overtook me. "Heavenly Father, I can't take any more of this. At least give me some kind of sign to show me that **You** still care," I pleaded.

When I arrived home, I sat down on the couch and began watching the *700 Club*. At the end of the program when they prayed, I bowed my head, shut my eyes, and prayed with them. During the prayer, I suddenly heard what sounded like a deep growl come from the corner of the room to my left. I opened my eyes but could see nothing there.

After the *700 Club* ended, I began channel surfing and discovered that the Gospel Music Association's Dove Awards were being televised. Before a commercial break, it was announced that up next, for the first time ever, was Third Day's new video. Third Day was my favorite band and my inspiration for learning the guitar, so I was excited to hear their new song for the first time. The title of the song was "Call My Name," and as it played, I sat frozen with tears streaming down my face. It was as if the words of the song were a message to me directly from God

Himself. It was obvious to me that this was God's answer to my prayer for a sign that He still cared. The moment was so surreal that it seemed like the Holy Spirit had given Third Day's lead singer, Mac Powell, the words to the song, knowing that on April 23, 2008, I was going to need to hear them.

* * *

THAT EXPERIENCE WAS one of those rare and cherished spiritual moments that a person never forgets, and I felt my faith was strengthened. Satan, however, was still going to make his presence felt.

Throughout the rest of the Dove Awards there was a tribute to Michael W. Smith, and more worship songs were sung. As the song "Agnes Dei" (Lamb of God) played, I sat on the floor with my eyes shut, singing along, completely in a spirit of worship, when suddenly I heard a loud growl that seemed to surround me. I couldn't pinpoint what direction the growl came from, as it seemed to come from every direction at once! Strengthened by the night's earlier events, I refused to even open my eyes and acknowledge the enemy's attempt at intimidation.

"Don't you even think you're going to interrupt my time of worship," I thought to myself as I then continued singing along as though I hadn't heard the growl.

Looking back, God was giving me a glimmer of hope that He cared, even though my nightmare was nowhere near being over yet. I kept praying and asking God to deliver me, and I kept binding demons. It became a daily ritual. As part of my prayers, I would bind demons, plead the blood of Jesus over the entire property, and break any curses I suspected were against me. I still had no idea what those curses might be, so I wasn't being specific, but I prayed in faith.

# CHAPTER EIGHTEEN

## THE DEVIL'S APPLES

*I* decided that I needed to try to attend church more regularly, hoping that this would strengthen my faith and provide Christian fellowship. One Sunday morning Maggie acted as my alarm clock as she woke me with loud barking for no apparent reason. Although I didn't usually sleep well, I was now wide-awake, so I decided to drive to a small Nazarene church in Sugarcreek, which was located in Tuscarawas County. I got ready and started my drive through the twisting, turning back roads of Holmes County, when I began experiencing intense feelings of hopelessness and despair. The further I drove, the more intense the feelings became.

I became so overwhelmingly depressed that I couldn't even think clearly. I turned my car around and returned home. There, I sat in the living room, praying and literally begging God to take the horrible feelings away. They remained. Suddenly, my fight instinct overtook the depression, and I realized it was time to fight back in the authority God had given me, instead of begging **Him** to do everything for me.

"Satan, get out of my face! I take authority over you in the name of Jesus Christ, and I bind you and your demons and command you to get out of my face and stop oppressing me!" I spoke forcefully.

Almost immediately, the horrible feelings left me, and I could think clearly as the depression lifted. I felt bad that I had missed church because of this latest attack, but I was thankful I'd gotten a reprieve.

Later that evening, while standing in the kitchen, I suddenly felt the enemy once again make an appearance. This time, however, he chose a different approach. It's hard to explain, but I began feeling as though someone were standing right there negotiating with me. There was no oppression or hopelessness, but rather the feeling of an old friend offering help. "What has God done for you? Look how bad you're suffering. Look how lonely you are. God's not going to help you sell this house, but I will. I will give you whatever you want if you stop following God and follow me. I will give you another beautiful wife and *anything* else you want. Just follow me."

I believe the negotiation was happening spiritually, as I didn't hear an audible voice. Nevertheless, it was as real as if someone were standing right in front of me. As I pondered the offer momentarily, immediately my mind recalled something I'd heard Pastor Perry Stone say.

"All the devil's apples have worms in them," I heard Pastor Stone's voice echo from the recesses of my mind.

"Yeah, and tomorrow you'll give me cancer, or make me get hit by a truck! I'm not that stupid. Get out of my face!" I answered the demonic presence that was trying to cut a deal for my soul.

Again, as had been the case earlier that day, the presence left after being rebuked. The following day, I spoke to the pastor of the church I'd attempted to attend. During our conversation, I explained that I'd gotten too overwhelmed while driving to church and returned home.

"I understand, Pat. I wish you could have heard my sermon though," he shared.

"I wish I could have heard it too. What was it about?" I asked.

"I preached about when Satan tempted Jesus," he replied.

With that answer, it became obvious why I'd been so oppressed when trying to go to church, and there was no way this could have been a coincidence. In the Gospel of Matthew, Satan tempted Jesus in almost the exact same manner that I had been tempted the previous evening.

*Matthew 8:8–11:*

*8 Again, the devil taketh him up into an exceeding high mountain, and sheweth him all the kingdoms of the world, and the glory of them;*

*9 And saith unto him, All these things will I give thee, if thou wilt fall down and worship me.*

*10 Then saith Jesus unto him, Get thee hence, Satan: for it is written, Thou shalt worship the Lord thy God, and him only shalt thou serve.*

*11 Then the devil leaveth him, and, behold, angels came and ministered unto him.*

I was thankful that my response was almost identical to what Jesus said to the devil. Telling the devil to "get out of my face" is a modern-day vernacular for Jesus' exact words, "get thee hence." Also, just as in the scriptural account, it had also been evident to me that the evil presence had left after I resisted. I was also thankful that although the enemy had caused me to miss a sermon that was completely relevant to the temptation I was about to face, the Holy Spirit had brought a timely reminder to me in the form of Perry Stone's words just when I needed it.

# CHAPTER NINETEEN

## SPRING & SUMMER 2008

The spring and summer seasons of 2008 were an emotional roller coaster. There were times I was able to tough it out with faith and hope, and times of total despair. When my listing contract with my Realtor ended that spring, I decided to list the property with a Realtor from Holmes County. I was hoping that maybe if I used a local Realtor, the Amish harassment would stop. The new Realtor's name was Jill, and I fully explained to her what I was dealing with, and how I'd been treated by the Amish. Jill was very pleasant and said she believed me and was aware of this type of activity in Holmes County.

"My husband's family is Amish, so I know what types of things *really* go on out here," she assured me.

Jill also asserted that my asking price was more than reasonable, and if the Amish tried to harass her, she'd have none of it. She even seemed unfazed by my reports of paranormal activity. I trusted Jill and believed that *finally* someone might actually have my back. After all, she now had a vested interest in my property selling.

That spring I also decided to open an online music store and began selling various guitars, effects pedals, and other musical instruments. At first the sales were very good, and I hoped this new venture would at least keep me afloat until the property sold.

As spring progressed to summer, more arduous circumstances surfaced. One morning when I went to the kennel to feed and water Maggie and Copper, I immediately noticed that Maggie was very sick. I rushed her to the vet, who ran a series of tests and diagnosed her with diabetes. The vet informed me that Maggie could have a normal life span, but treating her would be several hundred dollars per month. I was then asked if I wanted to put her down. I was devastated. Although I was already hurting financially, Maggie was just like a daughter to me. When friends and family were nowhere to be found, my pets always loved and appreciated me. I decided right then and there that Maggie deserved to live. Her care required special food and two insulin shots per day, but I was happy to be a blessing to her the way she was a blessing to me. I couldn't help but wonder, however, how much worse things could get for me.

Because my road still hadn't been paved, I decided to call Jim *again*, hoping that maybe this year they'd finally do the right thing.

"We can pave it for you if you pay us $1500. We're not doing any paving for *anyone* this year unless they pay us directly to do it," Jim said.

"Pay **you** for it? I pay my taxes, so you've already been paid to do it. Why should I pay you extra? You've paved a lot of other people's roads without charging them in addition to their taxes. Why is it different for me?" I fired back.

"There's no money to do anything but just repair the roads this year, so *nobody* is getting their road paved unless they pay extra," Jim explained.

"I'm sorry, but my dog got sick with diabetes, and I have to pay to treat her, so I don't have an extra $1500. Besides, I already paid for it to be done when I paid my taxes!"

"Well, we're not doing it for anyone unless they pay us $1500," Jim again asserted before hanging up.

Although Jim claimed that nobody would get their road paved unless they paid the extra money on top of their taxes, a few months later I saw that they'd paved the road in front of Eli's property. Suspecting this was once again a case of discrimination, I asked Eli if he'd had to pay Jim for paving the road for him.

"No. Jim did it for us for free," Eli answered.

"You're kidding me. He told me that he wouldn't pave my part of the road unless I paid him $1500! My house is never going to sell if they don't pave the road," I replied.

"Yeah, well, that wasn't right of Jim to do that," Eli said as he pretended to be upset with Jim.

This incident offered further proof of corruption in the local government of Holmes County and certainly pointed towards religious discrimination against me, because the trustees were clearly singling me out and catering to the Amish. It was becoming more obvious that the myth of the Amish mafia was, in fact, no myth at all. The Amish controlled *everything* in Holmes County, as far as I could tell, and anyone who didn't bow to them was marked and felt their wrath.

Late one night when I couldn't sleep, I was once again in the office when I heard a *very* loud noise that seemed to come from just outside the front of the house. It sounded like a loud crash as if something had just smashed my vehicle! Startled, I immediately dropped to the floor and crawled to the window. I looked out but saw no one, and nothing out of place. Suspecting that someone must have vandalized my vehicle, I got a flashlight and went outside, but found that nothing had been vandalized, and everything was eerily silent. I was never able to find an explanation for the loud crashing sound and eventually filed it away with the other strange experiences.

On one sunny afternoon, as I entered the foyer from the kitchen, I began hearing a strange scratching sound in the front wall beside the door. I slowly approached the wall and listened closely and determined that it was coming from the area right beside the light switch. I leaned forward and knocked on the wall right where the scratching sound was coming from, and it instantly stopped. A few seconds later the scratching started again, but this time it was in the upper left-hand corner of the front foyer wall, nearly twenty feet off the ground. There was no way a mouse or any rodent could have moved from the first location to the second, because there were studs and insulation behind the drywall, and there was no way anything could have climbed that high so quickly. Once again, I could find no explanation for this strange incident, but I was aware that scratching sounds in walls were occasionally experienced in haunted houses.

With each passing day being one step closer to the day I'd lose the house, the hopelessness and despair battled me almost constantly. Sadly, I also had *still* not really come to grips with the divorce, and I had never gotten closure. One afternoon, my old friend Ben called me and invited me to a revival at his father's church. Knowing I was desperate for a move of God, I decided I had to go. The first couple of nights, ministers prayed over me during the prayer time at the end of the service, and I felt the depression lift. When I returned home, however, the horrid feelings returned seemingly stronger than before. I continued going to the revival for several more services, but eventually my terrible circumstances weighed so heavily on my mind that I felt I had a dark cloud over me when I tried to pray or worship. The revival had strengthened me temporarily, but the oppression was now as bad as ever, and I felt like I was trapped in a nightmare I'd never escape. It was all I could do to keep mustering the strength to pray and have even a small amount of faith.

# CHAPTER TWENTY

## WITCHCRAFT!

*O*ne beautiful summer day, as I was once again working in the yard, I suddenly had what I believe was a revelation from God. As I was looking across the beautiful landscape, out of nowhere this thought entered my mind, *"They're practicing witchcraft!"*

I had never heard anything about the Amish or Mennonites practicing witchcraft, but somehow I knew it was true, and the term *"old-world witchcraft"* kept running through my mind. Later, when I was speaking to Mom, I said, "I don't know how I know this, and I can't prove it, but the Amish are practicing witchcraft, and that's part of my problem!"

A short while later, Mom gave me the phone number of a man she'd met named Vernon, who was formerly Amish, but had left the religion after he became a born-again Christian.

"You've got to talk to this guy. I told him what you're going through, and he said he wants to talk to you," she said as she gave me the number.

I called Vernon and introduced myself, and we exchanged pleasantries. He then proceeded to explain how he'd become a born-again Christian and left the Amish religion and was subsequently shunned by most of his friends and family.

"The Amish call me 'the Deceiver' because I try to get others saved and out of that religion," he explained.

"Vernon, no offense, but I think it's a cult."

"It **is** a cult!" he readily agreed.

"And you might think I'm crazy, but I think they're into witchcraft."

"Who told you that?" Vernon asked in a suspicious tone.

"No one *told* me, but I think God *showed* me," I answered.

"Well, I can tell you for a fact that you're right! They do practice witchcraft! My own family does it! I tried to talk to my dad, and I told him that they need to stop, but he got mad at me and said, 'But it works!' I said, 'Of course it works! The devil has power too!' They hate me for becoming a born-again Christian, and they want nothing to do with me now," Vernon explained.

Vernon reiterated several more times during our conversation that witchcraft is commonplace among the Amish and that, although they claim to follow the Bible, the Amish religion is **not** Christian. After my conversation with Vernon, I did a little more research and discovered that witchcraft among the Amish is *very* well documented, especially, but not limited to, a form known as POW-WOW. Not so coincidentally, I also learned that pow-wow is a mixture of *"old-world witchcraft"* and Native American witchcraft.

I theorized that if witchcraft was common among the Amish and I lived in the second-largest population of Amish in the entire world, then quite possibly *this* was the reason for the severe oppression and paranormal activity I was experiencing. But could the evil being done by others have such a drastic and negative effect on me as a Christian, simply because I lived an area that was a stronghold of demonic activity? If that was the case, did I have any hope of overcoming the stronghold that seemed to have me bound? Each new clue brought a slew of new questions, which only made the nightmare more convoluted and hopeless with each passing day.

# CHAPTER TWENTY-ONE

## A MEETING WITH THE REAL EXORCIST!

By October, my situation wasn't getting any better, but I got a glimmer of hope one day when I got my mail. I received a notification that well-known exorcist Bob Larson was coming to Canton, Ohio, for a spiritual warfare seminar and private counseling. At first I put it off, but as time wore on, I began wondering if maybe the problem wasn't the house at all! What if the problem was me? What if *I* was possessed? But could I even cast demons out of someone else if I was? It would cost $500 for an hour-long counseling session with Mr. Larson, but compared to what I was going to lose if my situation didn't change, that seemed like nothing. Besides, if I did need an exorcism, I was never going to be able to move forward in my life without it. Desperate for help, I called and scheduled my meeting.

On Wednesday, October 15, at the McKinley Grand Hotel in Canton, I met with Bob Larson, Pastor Louis Roy, and another man who was assisting them. I had to fill out several questionnaires to help pinpoint any spiritual issues I might be struggling with. Mr. Larson seemed very kind and patient as I explained not only my father's murder, but also my fairly recent divorce, and the paranormal activity and oppression that plagued my house. He then led me in prayers of renunciation and curse breaking, and then tried to provoke any demons that might be present in me. When he began rebuking and provoking demons, I felt the Holy Spirit rising up in me just like when I did an exorcism on someone else. Nothing manifested in me, but I did feel that the Holy Spirit confirmed that part of my problem was that I was struggling in my faith during times of severe oppression. The demons possessing my house were feeding off of this.

While I was explaining to Mr. Larson about the activity in my house, I said, "I live in the second-largest population of Amish in the entire world. I don't know if you know this, but the Amish religion is somewhat *dark*."

I was trying to put it nicely that they practice witchcraft without offending anyone present. With that statement, Mr. Larson piped up, "You aren't kidding it's dark! The roots of that religion are full of witchcraft and sorcery! Why do you think they put hex signs on their barns?"

I felt a sigh of relief that he knew about the witchcraft practiced among the Amish. I then explained that I prayed daily, bound demons, and pleaded the blood of Jesus over not only myself, but also my pets and property.

"Have you walked your property and taken authority and anointed it with oil?" he asked.

"Yes, I've done that several times already, but I can do it again," I answered.

"Listen, do all of that again, but I'm going to be honest with you. There may be only so much you can do because of the area where you live," he warned.

When Bob Larson acknowledged that the Amish witchcraft could be so prevalent in Holmes County that I might not be able to get complete deliverance, it spoke volumes about the depths of the wickedness I was facing! I was determined to once again walk the property, anoint everything with oil, and take authority. I also was relieved that the problem wasn't that I was possessed, although that might have had an easier solution.

Later that evening, I also attended the Spiritual Freedom seminar, and Bob Larson again attempted to provoke any demons that might be present in me, but to no avail. Later, Pastor Louis Roy also prayed with me and helped me work through some lingering issues from my divorce. All in all, I didn't regret spending $500 for the counseling and advice, because I trusted Bob Larson and knew he was very knowledgeable about spiritual warfare.

When I returned home late that night, I decided to bring Maggie and Copper into the garage to sleep. While letting Maggie run a little, I prayed standing in front of the house. Suddenly I heard again what sounded like a loud growl, but this time it seemed to come from the road out in front of the house. I opened my eyes, but could see nothing that would offer an explanation. At the time, Maggie was on the porch behind me and didn't react, but perhaps it was because the sound came from off in the distance.

A couple of days later, I again walked my entire property, anointed everything with oil, and prayed. In Jesus' name I generically broke every curse and commanded the demons to leave. I then anointed the doors of my house as well. I had done all this before, but I hoped it would be different this time. But what if Bob Larson was right, and there was only so much I could do because of the prevalence of witchcraft in the area surrounding me? I was a little hopeful considering that the strange growl I'd heard after returning home seemed to come from just beyond my property line. Maybe that was a sign the spirits were finally leaving. Only time would tell.

The following Sunday morning I decided to attend a church

in Berlin, Ohio. At the end of the service, I went forward for prayer. As I was praying, a man and woman came and prayed with me. The woman's name was Gina, and she claimed to have a prophetic gift and said that while the other gentleman was praying for me, she could see God was speaking things directly to my spirit.

"Well, I met with Bob Larson a few days ago because I'm having a lot of demonic oppression," I shared.

"Oh, I went through that myself a few years ago," she answered.

"Wait, are you talking about just *feeling* oppressed, or are you talking about paranormal activity?" I asked.

"Both! When I was a young girl, I lived in Nepal, and without knowing any better, I did Buddhist prayer circles. That opened doors to demon spirits. Then around thirty years later, the demons began tormenting me. I kept praying about it, and God showed me that I had to renounce Buddhism. When I did, it all stopped. If you keep praying, God will show you why you're being oppressed," she explained.

"I've been praying, and I know several things that could be contributing to the oppression, but I can't get it to stop. It's to the point now that I'm more angry than scared," I explained.

"That's a good sign. That means you're getting closer to your answer," Gina assured me.

When I returned home after church, I decided to do some laundry. As I was putting a load of towels into the washing machine, I called Mom and began telling her what Gina had told me. I had the washer set to cold water, and it was filling, when I began noticing hot steam coming from the open lid. I stuck my hand into the water and discovered it was extremely hot! I double-checked the heat setting, and it was set to cold water, so I turned the heat dial to hot and then back to cold, and the water turned cold. I found it very strange that this happened while I was explaining what Gina had told me.

I later related the incident to several different plumbers, and none of them could explain how this could have happened. I believe this incident showed that the demons were reacting to the idea that I might be getting closer to the answers I desperately needed.

# CHAPTER TWENTY-TWO

## PARANORMAL ACCIDENT

On Saturday, December 20, 2008, I had yet another incident that demonstrated just how vast the demonic network I was facing really was. I was working late that evening at my job as a security specialist and was in my office monitoring the premises. At approximately 10:30 p.m., I received a call from the company who monitored all the alarms for the building, and was notified that a rear door in one of the receiving areas had been opened, triggering an alarm. I instantly checked the interior security camera and could see no one near that door or even in that area.

Suspecting that someone was trying to break in from the exterior, I immediately left my office, exited the building, and ran around the perimeter to the door in question. No one was there, and everything seemed quiet and peaceful. Although it was a cold evening, there had been no snowfall and the ground was clear. I returned to my office, curious as to what might have triggered the alarm.

Approximately twenty-five minutes later, I received yet another phone call from the alarm company notifying me that *again* the same rear door had been opened, triggering the alarm. I was monitoring this door from an inside camera, and again there had been no one in the area, but I did notice that the exterior motion sensor light was now on. Again, suspecting someone was trying to enter the building through that rear door, I left my office and exited the building. During the last twenty-five minutes, there had been a substantial amount of snowfall. Anticipating that I'd find someone breaking in, I ran full speed around the perimeter of the building while also calling the police department on my cell phone. Without warning, I stepped on a sheet of black ice that had not been there on my first trip around the building. My feet went out from under me, and I fell very hard on the ice. When I landed, I knew I was hurt, but my adrenalin was masking some of the pain. I got up and regained my composure and went to the rear door where the alarm had been triggered. Not only was no one there, but there were no footprints in the snow other than mine.

Later medical examinations, including X-rays and an MRI, indicated that I'd sustained several injuries, including whiplash, a torn disc, a bulging disc, and a separated sacrum.

The following Monday, the alarm company sent repairmen to check the alarm on the rear receiving door that had twice been triggered the previous Saturday evening. I went to the area and spoke directly to the repairmen, who thoroughly checked the alarm wiring and keypad. They assured me that the alarm was **not** malfunctioning and was in perfect working order. They then showed me that the door would have needed to be opened several inches before the sensors would trigger the alarm. After a thorough investigation, I had no choice but to conclude that this accident had happened via a series of paranormal incidents. Sadly, with these new injuries, I now had to deal with another set of problems.

# CHAPTER TWENTY-THREE

## ADDING INSULT TO INJURY

*A*s I prepared for the Christmas holidays, it was unbelievably difficult to muster hope that my situation would get any better. As if my other problems weren't enough, I now had painful injuries to cope with, but because I had house payments to make, I kept working regardless. On December 29, when I returned home from work around 10:40 p.m., I went right to my bedroom and checked my answering machine. What I heard was beyond what I could believe. Although I hadn't spoken to Abe for several years, I'd received a message from him approximately fifteen minutes before I arrived home, and what he had to say was quite disturbing.

"Hello, Pat. This is Abe. I want you to come talk to me. My father wasn't murdered like yours was, but I was raped when I was young. It was awful. I was terribly raped."

Why in the world would Abe call me and tell me something like this when I hadn't spoken to him for years? We weren't on good terms by any means either! Was this some kind of sick game? I felt bad for him if he had been raped, but I wanted nothing to do with him because of his perverted and voyeuristic behavior!

I'd had enough. This time I was going to make sure the sheriff took me seriously! I called and reported the harassment and said I wanted a deputy to come to my house. I then got out my double-barrel shotgun and loaded it. When the female deputy finally arrived and rang the doorbell, I answered the door holding the shotgun.

"Well, now that you're here, I guess I won't be needing this," I said as I cracked open the barrel and removed the shells in front of her.

"Listen, I am sick and tired of the harassment I'm going through out here from the Amish. I want you to finally do your job!" I insisted.

I then invited the deputy inside and played the message for her. When the message was over, I explained, "This guy is a nutjob! He sneaks into people's houses and hides and watches them. He is a voyeur. I have warned him before to never come around here or else, and now he calls me out of the blue and leaves me a message like this? I want charges filed against him for harassment, and if you can get him to tell you who raped him, you need to charge them as well!"

The deputy didn't seem too keen on doing much, but she did agree to talk to Abe. After she left, I watched as she drove the cruiser to Abe's parents' house and made her way up their long drive. When she reached the top, the house then became lit up. Several minutes later the deputy left their house and called to inform me that Abe had been warned not to bother me anymore. She also noted that Abe didn't want to tell who'd raped him. I wasn't happy that he wasn't getting prosecuted, but I hoped the deputy's warning would curb any further harassment.

I had a very eerie feeling of being watched the rest of the evening. I went to the office and set my shotgun on the floor. I was trying to unwind when I heard a loud groan come from the foyer, just outside the office door! It sounded like a man's voice echoing through the foyer. I immediately picked up the shotgun and went to investigate, but found no one there. Just as a precaution, I then went to all the windows and opened the drapes and walked around in front of the windows, holding the gun. If someone was watching me from outside the house, I wanted to make it clear what they'd be up against if this continued. The fact that the strange voice seemed to come from the foyer left me feeling unsettled.

Everything seemed to calm down for a few weeks, but that wouldn't remain the case. Late in the evening, on Sunday, January 18, 2009, I found that Abe was up to his old tricks again. When I took my trash to the end of my driveway for pickup the next day, I decided to check my mailbox and discovered that Abe had left a letter for me. There were no new tire tracks or footprints in the snow, but the letter had no postage, so it hadn't gone through the postal service. The envelope had strange stickers of flowers that said things like "thinking of you," which made me now wonder if Abe was a homosexual.

In his letter he simply babbled on about not much of anything. He thanked me for some lemonade I'd brought the work crew one day while they were building my house seven years earlier, and said it was the best lemonade he'd ever had. He then asked strange questions about where I was working and where Chelsea lived now. This was clearly more harassment, and considering Abe was ignoring the deputy's warning to leave me alone, I felt as though I was being stalked. *Again,* I called the sheriff, and when a deputy arrived, I showed him the letter and demanded that charges be filed.

The deputy once again went to Abe's parents' house and told him not to contact me again. Just as before, the deputy ignored my wishes to file charges against Abe, so I called the sheriff and asked why.

"He has been warned repeatedly to leave me alone. He's not stable, in my opinion, and he has repeatedly ignored my warnings. This is nothing short of stalking, and I want charges filed!" I explained.

"Well, this isn't *really* stalking, and we told him not to do it anymore, so I'm not going to file charges," the sheriff defiantly responded.

"No, you're wrong! This *is* stalking! By the definition of the law, if he is causing me mental distress by contacting me after I told him to stop, it *is* stalking! I want charges filed! Furthermore, he tampered with my mailbox because he put the letter in there himself instead of sending it through the mail. Isn't it a crime to tamper with someone's mailbox?" I argued.

"Well, he didn't actually tamper with your mail itself because your mailbox was empty when he put the letter in it, so that's not a crime either," the sheriff claimed. It appeared that he was grasping for straws just to avoid doing his job.

"This is how it looks to me," I began. "You refuse to file charges on the Amish because you're an elected official. If you cross the Amish, you will get voted out at the next election. I'm a taxpaying citizen who is being harassed and stalked, but you don't care because I'm not Amish. I bet if I were Amish, and Abe's family were English, you'd file charges! You cater to the Amish! It is clear to me that Holmes County is run by a *cult*, and those of us who stand up to them are discriminated against. You need to do your job and protect and serve!" I snapped back before hanging up the phone.

The sheriff really didn't disagree that he was catering to the Amish so he could get re-elected, or that they controlled everything in Holmes County. He just refused to file charges no matter what I said. This was clearly corruption, but where could I go for help? The only person in the county whose authority overrode the sheriff was the coroner, and my case didn't apply for that type of intervention.

When I later obtained the police reports for these complaints, I found that the deputy's reports weren't completely accurate either. They never mentioned that I insisted on filing charges, and what they wrote in their reports was not truthful. They downplayed these incidents and made it appear that Abe was a caring neighbor instead of a troublemaking nuisance. In the case of the second incident on January 18, the deputy didn't even get Abe's name right. In his entire report he used the wrong last name. At the very least, this shows incompetence on the part of the sheriff's department, but I believe the greater issue goes much deeper than that.

It's virtually impossible to overstate how hard it was to even attempt to forgive people who continually harassed and tormented me. I knew, however, that harboring unforgiveness and rage would certainly leave me vulnerable for demons to continue their assault against me. This left me continually praying for the grace to do what I was unable to do on my own.

# CHAPTER TWENTY-FOUR

## HEXED!

*I*t was now 2009, and things were not looking up. I tried my best to put the bad situations behind me, but it seemed like every time I turned around, I was still tormented by my neighbors or the paranormal. At least my online guitar store was producing sales. People all over the world were buying guitar accessories from me, so I had a glimmer of hope that my new business might take off.

One day while driving to work, I noticed that Eli had hung a skull of a bull steer from a tree at the edge of his property. The tree was just off the road and very close to the same spot where we'd found Copper years earlier (chapter 3). Although this did seem strange, I didn't give it much thought. A few weeks later, however, I began getting notices from customers in different parts of the world, saying that they weren't receiving their orders. Customers from France, Italy, Spain and Brazil were all saying the same thing.

And to make matters worse, PayPal was refunding their money, so I was out the merchandise, money, and international shipping expenses. If this continued, it would sink me very quickly! I would have suspected it was some kind of online scam involving eBay, but considering the customers were all from different countries, I couldn't see how the incidents could be related. As I wondered if things could possibly get any worse, it occurred to me that there might be some correlation between Eli hanging the cow skull from a tree, and my strange run of bad "*luck.*"

As I wondered why would anyone want to hang an animal skull from a tree at the edge of his property, a crazy notion crossed my mind. Could it be that Eli was a witch?

One thing was certain, even though he acted pleasant to my face, Eli was not my friend and couldn't be trusted. As I thought on these things, I remembered how Maggie, even though she was inside the garage and would not have been able to see or hear him, had become very aggressive on that cold snowy day in February 2007 when Eli approached me on his bike (chapter 8). Animals can see and hear things that humans can't, and the way Maggie had become so agitated, I couldn't help but wonder if she was reacting to something dark from the spiritual realm that was attached to Eli.

My mind then drifted back to the incident in November 2007, in which I saw the black shadow behind me in my reflection in the window, the night *before* my Realtor signs were smashed, and immediately *after* I told Eli that an Indian man expressed interest in my house (chapter 13). There was no question in my mind that Eli was in some way involved in that incident. I theorized that if he was in fact practicing some type of witchcraft and had put a curse on me, this could possibly account for the inexplicable black shadow I'd seen behind me in my reflection.

I began doing research on various forms of witchcraft and discovered that witches will sometimes hang the skull of a bull steer from a tree on their property, as a sign to others that he or she is a witch. Furthermore, I also decided to research what types of curses might involve hanging a skull from a tree. I discovered that in a form of witchcraft known as Odinism, witches would hang animal skulls near the edge of their property to curse their neighbors. From what I could tell, in Odinism usually horse skulls were used, but I also discovered that Odinism is a very old form of witchcraft from Germany, which is where the Amish's ancestors came from. I also knew that just as in pow-wow, the Amish sometimes mixed the old-world witchcraft of their ancestors with other forms of witchcraft. I can't say for certain if Eli or other Amish near me were practicing Odinism, but the skull hanging from a tree on his property was certainly a good indicator that he was practicing *some* form of witchcraft.

Out of desperation I contacted a Pentecostal preacher named James, from a small church in a nearby town. According to an old friend of mine, Pastor James believed in curses. I called him and explained my situation, and he agreed to meet with me. Although I was expecting some spiritual warfare prayers to be prayed over me, or possibly Pastor James coming to my property to pray over it, instead he just shared with me the theology of his particular denomination. He did, however, encourage me to keep the faith and pray in the spirit.

As our meeting was coming to a close, several other Christians arrived for a Bible study and invited me to stay. I did, and at the end of the meeting, they all prayed over me. Although they didn't know all the details of what I was going through, they did lay hands on me and pray for my situation in general. Within two days, I discovered that the cow skull had been removed from the tree on Eli's property, and the problems I was experiencing with my international sales ceased as well. Could it be that the timing of these incidents was coincidental, or is it more likely that the prayers of several Christians made the curse powerless? Looking back now, I have no choice but to believe that they are indeed related, and that I won a small victory thanks to the prayers of a faithful few.

*This is the skull I found hanging from a tree near the edge of my Amish neighbor's property.*

# CHAPTER TWENTY-FIVE

## FORGIVENESS

*I*t was now nearly six and a half years since the house had been built, and although we'd been told then that the road would soon be paved, there was no indication that it would be done this year either. I was well aware that Jim Yoder was using his position as township trustee to punish me for standing up to both the Amish and his cousin Jonus for his faulty building practices. As stated earlier, another township trustee had even told me that Jim didn't like me and brought my name up repeatedly in the trustee meetings. Knowing that the township's deliberate neglect of my road was making the sale of my property virtually impossible, it was extremely difficult for me not to harbor unforgiveness. What they were doing was certainly illegal and discriminatory, but where could I go for help? I'd already learned the hard way that corruption in Holmes County was the way things were done.

One evening, as I was flipping through channels, I stumbled upon an interview with a man named Bill Weise, who is the author of a book titled *23 Minutes in Hell*. In his book, he shares his testimony of having a vision or out-of-body experience in which he visited hell. As he shared in detail how terrible hell is, and the torment that is inflicted upon people who go there, I thought of my enemies who had truly wronged me, and how if they never repent, they are headed for eternity in hell. Even though I hated the things that had been done to me, I didn't want anyone to go there. Mr. Weise's testimony really shook me to my core. I also had to come to grips with the fact that God had commanded me to forgive, and if I refused, I also could end up in hell. I thought of Jim, but instead of feeling anger and hatred, I now felt compassion.

The next morning, when I exited the garage to go feed Maggie and Copper, I saw Jim standing near my front porch. Apparently, he had a package that wouldn't fit in my mailbox, so he brought it to the house. Without hesitation, I approached him and said, "Jim, I want you to know that if I've done anything to hurt you, I'm sorry and I ask you to forgive me. And I forgive you for anything you've done to me."

Jim looked at me for a second, and a look of relief came across his face as he responded, "You know what, we've all got to live here. You're right, it just ain't worth it."

At that moment it was like both of us had a weight taken off our shoulders. Several years of negative emotions seemed to dissolve. I had no idea if Jim would really treat me any differently after that, but I knew I had done the right thing, and I felt at peace.

Within a few months, the road in front of the house was finally paved. Obviously, Jim had put his ill feelings towards me behind him and had finally done the right thing. I was grateful! I later checked with the township and discovered that Jim had done away with all records regarding the paving of township roads. Technically, since a township trustee is an elected official and is accountable to the taxpayers, this is questionable at best. I believe Jim's actions demonstrated clearly that I *was* being discriminated against, and the paper trail had been destroyed. This was yet another example of the lack of integrity in the local government. I can say, however, that I do truly forgive Jim, and I saw firsthand that the power of forgiveness cannot be overstated.

# CHAPTER TWENTY-SIX

## SPRING & SUMMER 2009

ith 2009 well underway with no hope of the house or property selling, I decided to expand my internet music business in hopes of making more money to pay for the house. I decided to open a music store on the property and not only sell musical instruments, but also teach guitar lessons. It seemed like a crazy idea, but in Holmes County many Amish and Mennonite families have businesses at their homes, so I thought it might actually work. Because I ordered in a substantial inventory of musical instruments and supplies, Mom made me custom curtains to cover the vertical windows on each side of the front door of the house. The curtains attached to the steel frames around the windows with strong magnetic curtain rods, and the curtains themselves also had magnets sewn into the sides of them. These magnets held the curtains snugly to the steel frames of the windows so no one could see in.

I set up shop, and almost immediately new students began taking guitar lessons. Several of these students would play integral parts in several factors of the haunting. For instance, a couple of Mennonite boys named Miles and Maynard Schrock began taking guitar and banjo lessons, which gave me the opportunity to converse with their father, Monroe, when he brought them for lessons. Monroe had previously been Amish, but had left the church for a newer order Mennonite faith and often openly discussed the Amish religion with me. During one such discussion I shared with Monroe what I'd been going through the past several years involving the paranormal and also the ongoing torment from the Amish.

*After I opened the music store, I hung magnetic curtains over the vertical windows at the front door for privacy.*

Monroe had no qualms about declaring the Amish religion a

cult and stated that not only was witchcraft common among the Amish, but that it was actually taught in his former church by the bishop, who just so happened to be Jacob Troyer Senior. Monroe shared that he had practiced witchcraft himself as instructed by the Amish church. He stated that because of this, he'd become so demonized that after he became a Christian, he had to "reclaim the land" he'd given up to the devil through witchcraft.

Monroe also stated that not only was he taught witchcraft in the Amish church, but that the Christian concept of being "born again" was spoken against. Monroe shared that Bishop Troyer warned his church to stay away from people who had been born again, because they were "worse off now than they were before"!

"They can't even claim to be a Christian religion if they don't believe in being born again," I stated. "Jesus himself said that we *must* be born again to go to heaven" (John 3:3).

"I know! That's how messed up their teachings are," Monroe agreed.

As the conversation progressed, I shared my experiences regarding Isaac Raber, including the strange inexplicable shadow I'd seen just before he arrived to ask me for a free right-of-way years earlier (chapter 5). Upon hearing my account, Monroe assured me that Isaac was in fact a witch, and so was his daughter.

"Isaac's daughter has gotten so deep into witchcraft that she's lost her mind. They say she's crazy now, but I think it's really demon possession from all the witchcraft," Monroe proclaimed.

Monroe then went on to say that witchcraft was so prevalent in Holmes County that there was an Amish doctor who used to live in Winesburg, who went as far as practicing soul travel (aka astral projection) in order to keep a watch on his patients.

"He could tell me things that happened in my house that he had no way of knowing. He could even tell me what was in my refrigerator. He was treating my daughter and had her on a special diet, and he accused me of feeding her things that he'd forbidden. He knew what was in my house and cupboards even though he hadn't been there!" Monroe assured me.

I was thankful for the insight Monroe offered from his many years in the Amish religion. Once again, my hunches had proved pretty accurate, and I wasn't crazy. At the very least, this gave me peace of mind and helped me to trust my discernment.

One sunny Saturday afternoon, a man and woman stopped by and inquired about guitar lessons. They seemed friendly enough and were eager to get started. The man's name was Doc and his girlfriend was Sarah. Doc was talkative, but Sarah said little that day. Before I knew it, they were not only taking lessons themselves, but they were bringing along friends who wanted to learn as well. One such friend was a woman named Becky. Doc, Sarah and Becky became regular students and were pleasant to teach. As time wore on, and the three of them became witnesses to the paranormal activity in the house, I felt I had to share my story with them. Doc had a healthy level of skepticism, but Becky and especially Sarah were believers. Sarah, in fact, claimed to have experienced the paranormal years earlier, and said she had gotten a very strange feeling the first time she and Doc had entered my house. I guess that explained why she was so quiet the day they stopped to inquire about lessons.

"I couldn't understand why I felt so creeped out in your house that day. It was a beautiful newer home and a sunny afternoon, but I had an uncomfortable and eerie feeling. I guess I was sensing something that's in the house," she explained.

Late one summer night, as I was making my rounds before going to bed, I happened to look out the front door while passing through the foyer. To my surprise, I saw that although it was very dark outside, everything around my vehicle was brightly illuminated. The only explanation I could come up with was that the lights on the front of the garage had been left on. I was certain, however, that I'd turned them off when I locked the garage door. I immediately went to the garage and discovered that the lights were indeed turned off. Just to double-check, I flipped the switch and could see through the side garage window that they turned on. I turned them back off, relocked the garage door, and went back to the foyer. I again looked out the door, and this time everything was dark and there was no light around my vehicle. There was no explanation for the mysterious bright light I'd seen illuminating my vehicle. Either the garage lights had inexplicably been turned on and then back off, or something else had illuminated the area around my vehicle supernaturally. Either way the incident was paranormal!

The next day, I couldn't stop thinking about this incident. I decided to double-check the vehicle records and discovered that after the divorce, the title had never been changed to my name. For over two years I'd been driving a vehicle with Chelsea's name on the title! I quickly got the title changed, but I couldn't help but wonder if the strange incident was related in some way to the car not being in my name.

I did my best to hide it, but I was *still* plagued by depression and hopelessness. The despair was often overwhelming. When I'd try to go to church, it would often escalate. Many evenings I would return home after working, and simply sit in a pitch-dark room, soaking in a plethora of negative emotions. This would occasionally lead me into periods of anger for which I'd later have to repent. I'd question how God could let me suffer like this, and what I could have ever done to deserve the events of the previous few years. Why would God have even let me be born just to suffer like this? It all seems childish and immature now, but at the time I wondered how this could possibly be fair. After all, I had been a faithful husband, faithful in my tithes, and I'd tried to follow God to the best of my ability, yet I had already lost my marriage, was always on the verge of potentially losing my home, and I always felt alone. If God cared about me, where were my Christian friends?

Furthermore, it had been over two years since my divorce, and it didn't seem like I would ever meet anyone else. It all was a tough pill to swallow, and it seemed like the so-called happy times I'd experienced years earlier were merely an illusion that I had been a fool to believe were real. Looking back now, I can see that this was not normal depression I was experiencing, but rather extreme demonic *oppression* resulting from the environment in which I lived. It was only by the grace of God that during these times, I was able to have a tiny shred of faith and pick myself up and keep fighting.

I'd lost hope that the property would sell, so I began thinking of ways to make the beautiful land profitable. After doing a little research on what types of businesses might prosper in the area, I decided to try opening a flea market on the land. I mowed the back four acres, made some signs, and set up some small booths. Even this new endeavor, however, seemed to come under strange paranormal attack.

For instance, I bought a new tent that had a steel frame. The bottom of each leg of the frame had a steel plate with a hole through it to drive the L-shaped steel tent rods through, to anchor it to the ground. One day while Mom, my sister Lory, and brother-in-law Matt were helping me prepare the flea market, Matt and I set up the new tent and securely anchored it down. I then left to go to work, but the others stayed behind. Hours later as they were leaving, Mom pulled out of the driveway and continued down the road when she happened to look back to the large field behind the house.

To her surprise, she noticed that the tent, which had been securely anchored down, was now collapsed and far away from where it had been set up. The three of them quickly returned to the field and found that not only was the tent now far from its original location, but its steel legs had been twisted and bent, and the steel rods that had anchored them down were missing. Assuming a powerful gust of wind must have collapsed the tent and blown it far into the field, they quickly began looking around for the steel rods because they feared that if I hit them with my mower, it would ruin the blades. When their search efforts proved unsuccessful, Lory returned to the tent's original location and discovered that the rods were still driven deep into the ground exactly where we'd originally placed them! Considering that these rods had been driven *through* holes in the steel plates at the bottom of the tent's legs, it's impossible for the tent to have been moved without pulling out the rods! There was no rational explanation for this, and everyone agreed that the incident was paranormal!

Mom and Lory often worked the flea market and music store while I worked my regular job, and both experienced uncomfortable and startling incidents while alone at the property. One afternoon, as Lory was leaving, she exited out the back patio door. As she was locking up, Maggie, who was in the kennel overlooking the backyard, began barking aggressively.

"It's just me, Maggie!" Lory called out, but as she turned to look, she realized Maggie wasn't looking at her. Instead she was looking down the grassy strip of land between the house and property line. Although Lory thought this was strange, she continued down the sidewalk. As she was walking, she happened to glance up and saw a man in strange clothes standing just beyond a small tree in the grassy area where Maggie had directed her attention. Startled, she did a double take and he was gone!

"He was wearing clothes from another time! He had on high boots and was wearing a floppy, strange-looking hat!" Lory recounted.

"Remember the hat Mr. Edwards wore on *Little House on the Prairie*? That's what the hat reminded me of. And he just vanished in a split second! I was really freaked out and felt like I couldn't get out of there fast enough!" she added.

I had experienced many strange occurrences, but what Lory was describing was a full-body apparition! It was no wonder she was scared! After the incident, I prayed more but still couldn't unlock the secret of the haunting.

Something positive did happen towards the end of that summer when I met a nice Christian woman named Rebecca at Pastor James' church. We seemed to hit it off well, and although I knew I risked scaring her off, I told her of the strange paranormal incidents that had plagued me the last several years. Rebecca believed me and became a very supportive and understanding friend, who always made time to listen when I needed to vent. She was a much-needed breath of fresh air! In the back of my mind, however, I suspected this was all too good to really be true.

On Labor Day, as the summer was drawing to a close, I held a bluegrass festival on the property and charged admission. I hired several bluegrass and folk bands, including some made up of Amish and former Amish musicians. I then booked some vendors, whom I charged for booth space. The event made for a fun-filled day, but I was once again reminded of the nuisances Abe and his brother Eli chose to be. As though I'd never called the sheriff on Abe or given him trespass warnings, he showed up at the festival and acted as though he had a right to be there. Because I didn't want to cause a scene, I merely kept him under surveillance instead of confronting him again. Although Eli always pretended to be my friend, he opened his field to Amish who wanted to see the bands but didn't want to pay admission. To make matters worse, when the event ended, *none* of the vendors paid me for their booths! I guess the way things had gone the past few years, I should have expected as much.

Not so coincidentally, one of the singers I hired for the festival was a man named David Byler, who had left the Amish church after becoming a born-again Christian. David's wife was still Amish, and he told me that he was being tormented greatly by the Amish because he'd left the church. He also told me in no uncertain terms that he believed the religion was a cult and that he experienced overwhelming demonic oppression after he stood up to them. I empathized with David and found it interesting that people who could substantiate my suspicions kept crossing my path.

# CHAPTER TWENTY-SEVEN

## A TIME OF FASTING

*As* summer faded into early fall, I again evaluated my situation. For the life of me I couldn't understand why I couldn't get my nightmare to end. The flea market and bluegrass festival hadn't proven to be lucrative enough to change my situation or even offer hope for the following summer. I had to be brutally honest with myself and recognize that I might lose the house and property long before then.

It was now nearly eight years since I'd purchased the land, and that September marked seven years since the house had been completed and I'd moved in. During that time, I'd lost my marriage, had two strange accidents causing serious injuries, and I'd experienced the paranormal realm in ways I'd previously never imagined.

I decided drastic measures needed to be taken spiritually. After learning the power of fasting in regards to spiritual warfare, I decided to set aside some time to fast and pray for a breakthrough. Beginning on September 11, I only drank water and didn't eat anything for around a day and a half. I concentrated on focusing on God and praying that He would intervene in the horrible circumstances that had me trapped. I hoped that at the end of the fast, I would see a major miracle take place right before my eyes. Although this didn't happen, when I look back now, I believe things were happening in the spiritual realm that I just couldn't see yet. It seemed that something had changed during that weekend, and I felt more empowered by the Holy Spirit. Experience had taught me, however, that a new attack of the enemy was probably on the horizon. I wanted to believe that I'd have the faith to endure this attack, if and when it came.

# CHAPTER TWENTY-EIGHT

## SOME NEW CLUES

One day, while discussing my situation with Rebecca, she suggested that I contact an evangelist she knew named David Schlabach, who was formerly Amish and had attended Pastor James' church. She said David lived not far from me and had mentioned before some of the strange things that secretly went on in the Amish community. I got David's phone number and called him. I introduced myself and explained the reason for my call and who'd recommended that I speak to him. He was a very friendly and understanding individual, who seemed to believe everything I told him, so out of desperation, I spilled my guts.

"David, it's hard to know where to begin. I've had all sorts of paranormal experiences, including seeing dark shadows out of the corner of my eye, and seeing these shadows move across the room. I've even seen them behind me in my reflection, and then they disappear. I've seen my pets in the room when there weren't even really there, and I've had phone calls made from inside the house while I was sleeping and alone. I could go on and on." I took a deep breath and continued.

"I'm divorced now, and I believe that whatever is here

attacked my marriage. My wife's behavior became very strange and violent, and then she just left me and wanted a divorce. I've also been harassed mercilessly by the Amish, and I believe they're practicing witchcraft. I found a skull hanging from a tree on my Amish neighbor's property, and I've had some former Amish men confirm that my witchcraft suspicions are valid. The oppression and depression I feel is overwhelming. I'm a Christian, and I've even performed exorcisms before, but I can't make whatever is here leave! This has gone on for years, and at times I've really struggled in my faith because of this," I vented as David patiently listened.

"Patrick, you wouldn't believe it if I told you some of the things I know go on out there. There is witchcraft and abuse, and there are a lot of suicides as well. Matter of fact, an Amish guy blew his head off just the other night outside Mount Eaton. I've had to cast demons out of some people too!" David shared.

After I explained to David the exact location of my property, things got even more interesting. "I know exactly where your property is located. In fact, when I was a boy, I used to farm the fields just over the hill from you."

David hesitated for a few moments and then continued, "Have you ever heard of Amos Thompson? Your land used to be part of his farm."

"Yes, I've heard of Amos. I've always heard that he was a really nice guy, in fact. It seems like everyone who knew him always comments about how nice he was," I answered.

"When I was a boy, I'd be helping farm the fields near your property, and I used to hear Amos throwing fits of rage and screaming cuss words. He would be coming completely unglued. It was awful!" David recounted.

"Wow, I've never heard anything like that about him before. That kind of makes me wonder if he had demons too," I thought out loud.

"Undoubtedly he did!" David uttered confidently.

"Something else to consider is that the Indians who lived in this area camped all along your property. The creek just below your land was a good water source, so they set up camp all along your property and all the way up to where the Stark Wilderness Center is now," David revealed.

"I've never heard that before either, David," I answered in astonishment.

David thought for a minute and continued, "You know, the Indians were **not** Christian people. They were pagan and were into very evil and demonic things. They may have even killed people on your land. There's no telling what all they may have done there that's still affecting you today."

"I was thinking the same thing!" I answered. We then shifted gears and started discussing more about my Amish neighbors. "Do you know a man who lives near you named Isaac Raber?" David asked.

"Yes, I know Isaac. I've had a lot of problems with him. He asked me to *give* him a right-of-way that was the entire length of my property. I refused, and since then, I've had nothing but problems from him. I've actually been told that he and his daughter are both witches," I answered.

"Listen, I know things about Isaac that I'm not at liberty to share, but he is a very evil man. I know some of the things he's into, and he is terribly wicked!" David recounted as though he really wanted to share what he knew.

I respected David for keeping his word and not divulging information about Isaac, but I suspected that what he knew corroborated what I'd heard about him being a witch. As our conversation drew to a close, David promised to stop by my house as soon as possible to see what help he could offer.

After speaking to David, my head was spinning. I appreciated the new information, yet I struggled to get my mind around it all. I looked forward to the day he'd stop by to help, and I hoped it would be soon.

# CHAPTER TWENTY-NINE

## KNOCK, KNOCK!

*A*s autumn progressed, I did my best to keep hope. The change of seasons was a reminder of passing time and my nightmare dragging on. Although I was happy to be spending time with Rebecca, I still struggled with feelings of self-worthlessness. There was a very realistic chance I could lose my home in the not too distant future, and I felt like I wasn't being fair to her if we continued dating, knowing she could do better than a loser who was shouldering such a huge burden. Part of me wanted her to care no matter what may come, but part of me wanted to push her away. Multiple times I attempted to cancel dates at the last minute, but she was having none of it. Each time she'd still come to see me, which always lifted my spirits.

It was also during this time that in my desperation for answers, I finally began to take notice of a strange residue that was on the window of the front door of the house. I'd walked by and ignored it for a very long time, but now, the more I looked at it, I began seeing what looked like a face in the residue. For some reason, even though I knew it had basically always been there, I would never allow myself to question what it was or examine it. I guess I'd suspected it was residue from a sticker that must have been on the door when it was new. But why would it still be there now? It wasn't like we had neglected to wash the windows the entire time we'd lived in the house. In fact, when the house was first listed for sale and I began having open houses, Mom and Lory had washed the windows inside and out, so why would this residue keep reappearing? I didn't know what to make of it, but I suspected it could be relevant to the paranormal activity in my home.

One day in the beginning of October, I received an enthusiastic call from my Realtor, Jill. "Pat, there is a gentleman who wants to take a look at your back four acres behind your house. He seems really interested!"

"Is he Amish?" I instinctively asked.

"No, he's not Amish," she assured me. "He'd like to stop and look at the land Tuesday night if that's ok with you."

"I have people coming for guitar lessons Tuesday night, Jill," I answered.

"Don't worry about that. Go ahead with the lessons. I will take care of everything," she promised.

Selling four acres would have been helpful in my crisis considering that even in the current poor real estate market, the land was realistically worth $18,000 per acre.

The following Tuesday evening as I taught Doc, Sarah and Becky guitar lessons, the man came and looked at the property. Because I was busy with the lessons, I never saw him.

The next day Jill called me to discuss the potential sale. "Pat, he really liked your land and made an offer."

"Ok, what's his offer?" I asked.

"Don't be offended. It is a little low. He offered $12,000 per acre," she replied. Knowing the actual current value of the land, I immediately became suspicious, so I asked again, "Is he Amish?"

"No. He's not Amish," Jill again responded.

"Well, that offer is insulting. I'm willing to negotiate and be fair and reasonable, but if he's really interested, he needs to make a more realistic offer than that!" I said in disgust.

"Sometimes people just start out really low, Pat," Jill countered.

"Yeah, but that is one-third less than the current market value. Are you sure he's not Amish?" I again asked.

"I'm sure he's not Amish, Pat." she reassured me. "Oh, there is one more thing. His bank would like to come out and appraise your property," she added, seemingly as an afterthought. With that statement, I became even more suspicious.

"Wait a minute, Jill. That doesn't make sense to me. Since when does a bank appraise a property when a selling price hasn't even been agreed upon? His offer isn't even in the ballpark of what I'd consider, so why would a bank come and do an appraisal?"

"Well, it's not the norm, but sometimes banks do this," she assured me.

My skepticism grew. "Well, I'm not buying it. This makes no sense. Who is his bank?"

"The Amish Helps Fund," Jill reluctantly answered after a long pause.

Her answer revealed that she had been less than honest with me. The Amish Helps Fund is basically a bank that is over Amish and Mennonite churches, and it distributes loans to Amish and Mennonite families and businesses. The Amish and Mennonites pay into the fund via tithes into their churches.

"So he IS Amish?" I asked yet again, as I felt my anger kindling inside me.

"Yes. He's Amish," Jill answered after another pause. I realized that if I allowed the appraisal to be done, my land would likely be appraised far below what I knew its real market value to be. With the property being devalued, I would be forced to sell it at a greatly reduced price. I knew this was clearly another attempt by the "Amish mafia" to take my land by dishonest means. As was the case in my previous encounters with these scoundrels, I was having none of it.

"You go tell that **CULT** that I will **not** have my selling price dictated to me by a *cult!* Tell them what I said, and use those exact words!"

Jill agreed to tell them what I'd said, and we ended the call. As I hung up, I realized that now I couldn't even trust my Realtor. Anger and isolationism once again began to set in.

Later that evening, as I was channel surfing and trying to forget the intense burden I was carrying, I happened upon a Christian telethon on the Inspiration Channel. I stopped to listen for a few minutes. A well-known Christian author named Mike Murdock was speaking about the biblical principle of reaping and sowing, and how it relates to a Christian giving monetarily to ministries who further the Gospel.

As I listened, Mr. Murdock began sharing many stories of times in his life when he'd planted "seeds" of $1000 into others' ministries, and God immediately blessed him. I thought of all the thousands of dollars I'd given to the various churches I'd attended over the years, as well as ministries I'd supported financially. I thought of how I was on the verge of losing everything, and also about how horrible I felt about myself. Again, I began feeling anger rising in me.

"Well, I'm glad that worked out for you, Mike!" I shouted at the TV before shutting it off and throwing the remote control in disgust. I went to bed that night feeling forgotten and abandoned. Unable to sleep, I began watching a Christian DVD, hoping to find comfort and answers. The video I selected that night was a special teaching series from Pastor Perry Stone, titled *Purging Your House*, which dealt with spiritual warfare and cleansing your house of evil spirits.

At approximately 3:35 a.m., I was still unable to sleep and arose to use the bathroom at the top of the foyer stairs. I had been in the bathroom for a few minutes when I suddenly heard two loud knocks on the solid oak bathroom door!

I was so surprised, I started to answer "what?" as if someone else was actually there. Then, in a split second, I remembered that my doors were locked, and no one else knew the code to disarm the security system, so no person could have entered the house!

Immediately, sheer terror rushed through me! I tried to pray but was so shaken that nothing would come out of my mouth. It was as if I were in one of those terrible nightmares where you try to scream but can't. I, however, was very much awake. With all the strength I could muster, I tried to force words out of my mouth.

"I bind you in Jesus' name!" Although under normal circumstances that much effort would have produced a loud yell, barely a whisper came out! Nevertheless, I continued. What else could I do?

"I command you in Jesus' name to get out of my house! I bind you and command you to leave my house now!"

There were no other noises or disturbances, but whatever was haunting the house had achieved its goal. I was mortified. As I tried to gather my thoughts, I considered staying locked in the bathroom until sunrise a few hours later. It made perfect sense at the time, although looking back now, it seems illogical. A little after 4:00 a.m., I decided that I had to leave the bathroom and investigate the house, just to rule out if someone had actually somehow entered. I scoured through the linen closet, looking for anything I could use as a weapon if an intruder was present. Eventually, I found a pair of barber shears.

Gripping them tightly, I reached for the doorknob. Before opening the door, I took a few moments and cemented in my mind that no matter what I saw when I opened the door, running was *not* an option. You can't run from a spirit, and you can't fight it with physical strength or a weapon. I resolved that no matter what

I saw, no matter how horrifying, I would run *towards* it, quoting scripture and taking authority over it in Jesus' mighty name! If this thing wanted a fight, it was going to get it, come what may.

I gripped the doorknob and slowly opened the door and stepped out onto the landing at the top of the foyer stairs. There was dead silence. Praying along the way, I went to the bedroom and picked up the phone and called Mom as I grabbed my shotgun and began looking for my box of shells.

"Hello," Mom said in a tired voice.

"Mom, it's me. Something creepy just happened again. I was in the bathroom and something knocked twice on the bathroom door!" I said in a shaky voice.

"Those stinking demons!" Mom responded.

"I'm loading my shotgun, and I'm going to keep you on the phone while I walk through the house to make sure someone's not hiding in here!" I explained as I fumbled through the room. "Now where are those shells?"

"You're not going to need them, Patrick. You're dealing with a demon, not a person!" Mom assured me.

"I know you're right, Mom, but the knocks were so loud that I have to make sure someone isn't in the house," I replied as I located the shells and loaded my 20 gauge.

I then systematically searched the entire house, including the closets, only to discover my gut hunch was correct. No one was there! The doors were still locked and the security system still armed. I took notice that the horrifying incident just so happened to take place between 3:00 and 4:00 a.m., the witching hour.

I couldn't help but believe that the terrifying experience was directly related to the events of the previous day, in which I'd called out the Amish religion as a cult. Later that day, I called Jill and confirmed that she had indeed relayed my exact message to the Amish bank, as well as the potential buyer. I then explained the experience I'd had, and told her I believed it was directly related to me standing up to the Amish.

"Jill, I don't even care if you think I'm crazy. I just don't care anymore. I know what happened, and I know it came from them. I don't even want to sell the land to this guy. Forget it! Tell them to get lost and leave me alone. I will *not* deal with them!"

Jill tried to persuade me back to the bargaining table. "Pat, I believe you. I told you before that I know things like that go on out here, but I don't think you should just walk away from a potential sale."

"There is no bargaining. There's no negotiating. They're a crooked and corrupt cult. They think they control everything, like they're the mafia. Well, they're not controlling me. They can conjure up what they want against me, I won't back down!" I answered, standing my ground.

Jill finally agreed to tell them I wasn't interested in the sale, but she wasn't happy with me. The following day her business partner, Janine, called and gave me a tongue-lashing for not letting the Amish devalue my land so they could get it at a steal.

"You're supposed to be a Christian. You should forgive him instead of just walking away from the sale," she argued.

"Do you have things knocking on doors inside your house in the middle of the night after you stand up to them?" I asked rhetorically.

"I didn't think so. You and I both know that his so-called bank would have appraised my property low, which would have devalued it. And I am convinced that the incident I experienced in the middle of the night, after I stood my ground, came from them. I'm not dealing with them and their witchcraft. I don't care what anyone else thinks!" I retorted.

I ended the call very frustrated and disappointed. Clearly, Jill and Janine cared only about their commission, and not about me as their client. Again, I saw just how powerful the Amish church's influence was in Holmes County.

Just as before, after that incident when I tried to go to church, a deep depression and feeling of hopelessness would overtake me. I wondered how I could possibly overcome the odds I was facing. I knew it would only be by a miracle, and if that required me to have superhuman faith, I was likely going to fall short. Then I remembered that Jesus said if we have faith the size of a grain of mustard seed, we would, in effect, be able to speak and see the impossible come to pass (Matthew 17:20; Luke 17:6).

With that I prayed, "Lord, *You* said if I have faith the size of a grain of mustard seed, I could speak and move mountains and see trees uprooted and cast into the sea. Isn't the fact that I'm praying to **You** and asking **You** to help me proof that I at least have that tiny amount of faith? Please intervene."

# CHAPTER THIRTY

## A STEP OF FAITH

*A* few nights later on October 9, I turned on the TV and again happened upon the same telethon on the Inspiration Channel. Again, Mike Murdock was speaking about giving monetarily to further the Gospel. This time something was different. I sat quietly and listened as Mr. Murdock once again shared many stories of times he'd planted $1000 "seeds" into ministries, and how God blessed his faithfulness. As he continued speaking, he stated that he believed that God was telling him that there were people who were watching whom God was calling to give a gift of $1000 to Inspiration Ministries. In my state of desperation, what Mr. Murdock said next really got my attention.

> *"I believe that those who are obedient and pledge a $1000 seed into this ministry will receive three blessings for their obedience. One, God will give them favor with people who can help turn their situation around. Two, God will give them a hundredfold return on their $1000 seed. Three, God will give them ideas that will turn their situation around!"*

As I sat there in the living room of a house I might lose in the very near future, I trusted what Mike Murdock was saying. I felt strongly that God was asking me to step out in faith and pledge $1000. Considering my financial state, that was a huge commitment.

"What do I have to lose? At least if I give this money and still lose everything, I will always know I didn't go down without a fight! If I'm going down, I'm going down swinging!" I told myself as I picked up the phone, called Inspiration Ministries, and pledged $1000.

I felt peace about pledging the money. I truly believed God had called me to give, and even if I lost everything, I knew my step of faith was something I needed to do. Even though my faith had been a roller-coaster ride the last several years, I was going to fulfill my pledge and be obedient no matter what. The Bible says that faith without works is dead (James 2:20, 2:26), and I believe that pledging the $1,000 seed was a good work that I needed to do as a demonstration of my faith in God.

# CHAPTER THIRTY-ONE

On Sunday, October 18, While chatting with friends on Facebook, I received a friend request from a woman named Angie, whom I'd gone to grade school with, but hadn't spoken to in years. I accepted her request, and we chatted for a little while, catching up on where our life journeys had taken us over the last few decades. Eventually, the subject of our religious beliefs surfaced, and Angie stated that she and her husband, Dennis, were also born-again Christians. As our conversation progressed, I vented my frustrations about what I was experiencing in Holmes County.

"Angie, I know you're a Christian, but you may think I'm crazy if I tell you what I've been experiencing. My house is haunted, and I've been having all sorts of paranormal activity and demonic oppression for several years. My Amish neighbors torment me, and I think some of them are into witchcraft!" I explained.

Upon hearing that, Angie gave me her phone number and asked me to call her right away. When I did, I discovered that not only did she not think I was crazy, but she and Dennis had experienced the paranormal and spiritual warfare as well. After swapping several stories of our experiences, Angie asked where exactly in Holmes County my house was located. When I explained the location, things became even more interesting.

"Hmmm. Pat, I think Dennis grew up not far from you. He was adopted and raised by an Amish family, but he never joined their church. I really need to tell him what you're experiencing, and see if he has any insight about what's causing this. I'll let you know what he says," Angie explained.

"I greatly appreciate any help either of you can offer," I assured her as we ended our call. The following Sunday, I received the call back that Angie had promised.

"Pat, I talked to Dennis, and he thinks he has some clues that may help you. I'm going to let him tell you, because he can explain it better than I can," she announced. Angie handed Dennis the phone, and he introduced himself. He seemed like a friendly enough individual, and I couldn't wait to hear what these clues might be.

"Pat, Angie said that you think the Amish around you are practicing witchcraft, and that may be causing the oppression you're experiencing. I think you're right about the witchcraft, but you have a much bigger problem than that. Have you ever heard of the Greenville Treaty?" he asked.

"Not that I can remember," I answered.

"Hundreds of years ago, our government and the American Indians signed a treaty called the Greenville Treaty. The treaty line runs right by your property. After the Indians broke the treaty, the government rounded them up and shipped them out West. The Indians were so angry that they cursed all of the land. You built your house on cursed land, and that's why it's haunted!"

"You've got to be kidding me," I said in disbelief.

"No, I'm serious. I know about the curse because I was adopted and raised by an Amish family. The ancestors of the Amish were here when this all happened, and they passed the story down, from generation to generation. The Amish know all about this, but they're never going to tell you! I only know because I lived with them for many years," Dennis recounted.

"I've owned this land for eight years, and I've never heard that there is a treaty line near my property. This is all beginning to make sense, Dennis. I really appreciate you sharing this with me," I said as I struggled to get my mind around this new and somewhat intimidating piece of information.

"Pat, look it all up. The Greenville Treaty is a piece of American history. You'll see that the treaty line is very close to you. I know how the Amish can be, and I know many of them are into witchcraft, but I think this is a bigger problem for you. We will help you any way we can. Just let us know if you need anything," Dennis promised as we ended the call.

After our conversation, my thoughts were racing, and I knew I had to do more research on the Greenville Treaty. At the same time, however, I couldn't help but remember what Mike Murdock had said during the telethon on the Inspiration Channel (chapter 30). He'd stated that he believed that those who were faithful in giving to support that ministry would obtain favor with people who could turn their situation around. Could it be that Dennis and Angie were two such people? If so, could that mean that my situation was about to change?

# CHAPTER THIRTY-TWO

## THE GREENVILLE TREATY & INDIAN CURSES

*T*hat very afternoon, I began researching the Greenville Treaty and discovered that it was indeed an important chapter in America's history. In 1794, American forces led by "Mad Anthony" Wayne defeated the Indian forces at the Battle of Fallen Timbers. After this battle, a coalition of approximately twelve tribes, known as the Western Confederacy, agreed to the Greenville Treaty in August 1795. In exchange for $20,000 worth of goods and an additional $9500 in goods annually, the Indians turned over much of their territory in Ohio as well as other areas.

A treaty line was established separating the Native American territory from the land open to white settlers. The Greenville Treaty line began at the mouth of the Cuyahoga River (present-day Cleveland, Ohio) and ran southward through the Portage Lakes area (present-day Akron and Canton, Ohio) and continued south to Fort Laurens (present-day Bolivar, Ohio) and then turned southwest through Holmes County. Through more research and extensive map searches, I discovered that the Greenville Treaty line was, in fact, only a few hundred feet from my house.

As I thought about other ways this curse might play out in modern times, I found it intriguing that the cities of Cleveland, Akron, and Canton, Ohio, have some of the highest crime rates in the nation. Furthermore, the Bolivar area has high claims of paranormal and haunting activity. As I thought about how the treaty line ran through Holmes County, I also realized that Holmes County is, in my estimation, a cesspool of witchcraft, child abuse, incest, perversion and crime, all deceitfully cloaked in a supposedly peaceful religion. Was it a coincidence that all these areas touched by the Greenville Treaty line seemed to be cursed?

As I dug a little deeper into the Greenville Treaty, I also discovered that the great Shawnee Indian Chief Tecumseh had rejected the Greenville Treaty and refused to sign it. Later, with the help of his brother, who was known as "the Prophet," Tecumseh revolted against the American government. Much because of this revolt, the Native Americans were relocated to reservations between 1830 and 1850. It has been well documented that Indians did believe in cursing people, as well as territories they were giving up. Two such examples of this are "Tecumseh's Curse" (aka the Zero Year Curse) and "the Curse of Chief Cornstalk."

"Tecumseh's Curse" pronounced that William Henry Harrison and every United States president elected in the twentieth year after him would die in office. Tecumseh allegedly uttered the curse in 1811 after the Battle of Tippecanoe, and Harrison wasn't elected president until 1840, which was twenty-seven years after Tecumseh's death. Nevertheless, Harrison did die in office and was followed by Abraham Lincoln (elected in 1860), James Garfield (elected in 1880), William McKinley (elected in 1900), Warren Harding (elected in1920), Franklin Roosevelt (elected in 1940), and John Kennedy (elected in 1960). The curse only stopped when Ronald Reagan was elected in 1980, but well-known deliverance minister Derek Prince claimed to have recognized the legitimacy of the curse and broke it over Ronald Reagan and all future presidents.

"The Curse of Chief Cornstalk" has also played a significant role in the history of the region where it was pronounced. According to legend, in 1777 as Shawnee Chief Cornstalk lay dying from a murderous gunshot wound, he cursed the land that is now Point Pleasant, West Virginia. The significance of this curse is that Point Pleasant has been a hot spot for not only paranormal activity such as the Mothman, and UFO sightings in the 1960s, but also many horrific tragedies such as the Silver Bridge collapse of 1967, the worse coal mining disaster in American history in 1907, and multiple fatal plane crashes, etc. These tragedies certainly lend themselves to belief in the validity of "Cornstalk's Curse."

I dug a little more and found documentation stating that there were multiple incidents in Holmes County, where both Indians and white settlers crossed the Greenville Treaty line and were murdered. A couple of the incidents even involved children who had gotten lost and crossed the line accidentally. With my house so close to the treaty line, I couldn't help but wonder if anything like this had happened on what was now my property.

After doing a little research, I was beginning to think that Dennis might be onto something. I knew that there was no way to prove if the curse was real, but after everything I'd experienced the past several years, I felt compelled to take it seriously. Dennis certainly believed the legend that had been passed down through his adopted family for over two hundred years, and strangely enough, it all seemed to make sense.

It was unclear if someone such as Tecumseh had cursed the land right after the signing of the Greenville Treaty, or if other Indians did it later when they were relocated from Ohio to reservations in Kansas. At this point, however, all that really mattered was that the curse had to be broken in Jesus' name, using the Bible as my guide.

With these new clues, I again went to prayer. I was desperate for answers, so I began asking God to show me what exactly had caused the land to be cursed. I discerned very strongly in my spirit that not only had Native Americans cursed the land after the Greenville Treaty, but they had also murdered white settlers on the land that was now my property. The more I prayed, the more I became convinced of this. I began to have the same familiar feelings that I often experienced when doing exorcisms and discerning particular demon spirits. Strange intense chills ran across my upper back and down my arms as I asked God for answers. I believe this is one way the Holy Spirit manifests his presence in me when I'm doing spiritual warfare.

After praying, I felt like I now knew why I hadn't been able to get the haunting to stop. I hadn't really addressed the root of the problem. Sure, the Amish witchcraft was a reality, but if I wanted to overcome everything I was facing, I needed to specifically fight back against every form of evil that was tormenting me. According to Exorcist Bob Larson, the more specific you are at breaking a curse, the more complete the deliverance will be. That certainly appeared to be true in this case.

Later that evening, one of Eli and Anna Mae's cows got out and went far into the field just above my property. As Anna Mae was trying to round up the cow, I went out to see if I could help. As we were talking, I asked her what she knew about people being killed on our land.

"We know battles were fought here. Eli has found arrow heads different times when he's plowed," she answered.

"So people were killed here?" I again asked.

"Yes. There were battles fought here and people died," Anna Mae answered unequivocally.

As I walked back home after helping Anna Mae, I felt like the puzzle pieces were falling into place. With this new information, I believed that I needed some Christians to come and walk the entire property with me and pray and drive out whatever was there. This was something far too powerful for me to take on alone.

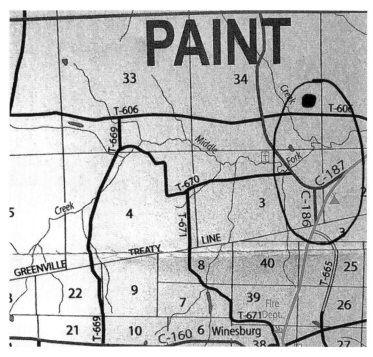

*This map of paint township in Holmes county shows where my house (marked with A black dot) was in relation to the Greenville Treaty line.*

## CHAPTER THIRTY-THREE

### THE HOWLING!

*E*arly one morning I was awakened by the sound of someone knocking on my front door. Because I usually didn't sleep that well, and I wasn't working until later that afternoon, I ignored the knocking and went back to sleep. Hours later after I had gotten up and went outside to feed Maggie and Copper, I noticed a note on the windshield of my vehicle. I went to investigate and discovered it was a business card from David Schlabach, with a note scrawled on the back. "Pat, I was here today and walked in your driveway and prayed. Call me!"

I felt some wind blow into my sails again. David had finally stopped by. I was kicking myself for not answering the door, but I was hopeful that help might be on the horizon. I quickly took care of Maggie and Copper and then returned to the house. I was excited as I entered and made my way into the foyer. There, however, my excitement turned to anger and fear. As I walked into the foyer, I noticed that the curtain covering the vertical window to the right of the front door had been moved inexplicably. The very top section of the curtain was moved, and the magnetic curtain rod at the top of the window had been manipulated so it was now at a strange angle, with the left side of the rod drastically lower than the right. Because the upper part of the curtain, which had been moved, was taller than I am (six feet four), and the rest of the curtain remained unmoved, it was impossible that Moses or Zoe could have done this. I could find no explanation for this strange occurrence and had to consider it paranormal! I found it peculiar that this occurred just after David had come to the property and prayed.

A short while later I called David on his cell phone and was shocked by what he shared. "Patrick, I believe I had something strange happen at your house today!"

"So did I, David. What was your experience?" I asked in anticipation.

"Well, let me ask you something before I say anything more. Do you have a dog that howls like a wolf?" he asked.

"No, David. I don't. I have a Rottweiler and a beagle. Neither howls like a wolf," I answered.

"Do any of your neighbors have a dog that howls like a wolf?" he asked.

"No, David. None of them do. Why are you asking me this?" I asked as a familiar, uncomfortable feeling swept over me.

"Listen, Patrick, you've got problems there. When I got out of my car in your driveway, I could feel the evil. I said out loud, 'You demons are going to leave him alone.' After I knocked on your door and didn't get an answer, I began walking in your driveway and praying. As soon as I started to pray, I began hearing a wolf howling. Part of me knew it was spiritual and not a real wolf, but I had to ask and make sure there wasn't a rational explanation," he recounted.

I then related my experience of the curtain and magnetic curtain rod moving inexplicably. After letting him digest that information, I continued and shared Dennis' claim of an Indian curse on the land. I couldn't help but notice that David's experience earlier that day seemed to validate Dennis' story, considering that wolves were often used as Native American symbols.

"Patrick, what you have going on there is *very* demonic. I will talk to my pastor and see what we can do to help you. I'll contact you again as soon as I can," David promised before hanging up.

# CHAPTER THIRTY-FOUR

## FREAKSHOW!

One day around a week later, as I was outside working in the yard, David again stopped by. He got out of his truck and introduced himself since it was our first time meeting in person. While we were talking, I decided to show him the strange residue on the window of the front door and get his opinion. When David stepped up onto the porch, he suddenly stopped.

"Patrick, I can feel something here as soon as I step foot on your porch."

We entered the house, and just as I was about to show him the window, he suddenly turned and looked around the foyer and interjected, "What is that?"

"What is what?" I asked.

"That noise. You don't hear it? It sounds like a loud whooshing sound," he explained.

"David, I don't hear anything," I replied.

He stood there listening with a puzzled expression on his face for a few moments and then commanded forcefully, "I rebuke you in Jesus' name. You stop that *NOW*!

"There, it stopped," he said as he redirected his attention to me. Although I hadn't heard anything, it would have been hypocritical of me to doubt David's word, considering all the experiences I'd had in the house. I then showed David the window of the front door.

"David, do you see a face in this residue on the window?" I asked.

"Yes, I see it," he replied.

"So this isn't just me thinking I see something that's not really there, right?"

"No, Pat—I can see it too," he confirmed. David then went on to explain that he'd spoken to his pastor about my situation, and that they wanted me to come to their church so they could pray over me.

"David, I'll come to your church, but that is **not** going to change my situation here. I've been to other churches, and they prayed for me too, and it did nothing to make the demons in my house leave. What I need is for other Christians to come here and walk the property with me and pray in agreement and drive the demons out, in Jesus' name. I know now that what's here is bigger and more powerful than what I can deal with on my own," I explained.

"Well, we'll pray over you, and when you come back home and step foot on this property, the demons will just flee from you," he claimed.

With that statement, I could feel the wind leaving my sails once again. How could it be that so many so-called Christians, including David's pastor, didn't understand simple biblical principles? Was I asking too much by wanting them to come to the property and help me?

Part of me suspected that David's pastor was more concerned with me attending their church than helping a fellow Christian in need. Unfortunately, I'd seen that before. In my desperation, I again agreed to come to their church the following Sunday morning.

Sunday morning, when I arrived at the small Pentecostal

church, David instantly greeted me and took me inside. He led me about halfway up the sanctuary, where we sat down at the end of a pew. Almost immediately, something didn't seem right, but I was desperate. I noticed that everyone kept giving me strange looks. When the worship time began, I tried to focus on worshipping God, even though the children of the church were yelling loudly and playing with toys in the aisleways.

At first, the worship team sang a few songs, such as "Revelation Song," but then the service took a strange twist. They began chanting a bizarre mantra.

"We cut off the devil's head, and we eat his head for bread!" they chanted over and over. As I watched what was quickly becoming a dog and pony show, I realized how important it is to have order in a church service. "I'm going back to the Nazarene church after this," I thought to myself.

After the chanting subsided, the preacher, Pastor Mark, stepped forward and announced that they had a guest this week. With that, David stood and ushered me to the front of the church. With everyone watching, they began asking me questions, some very personal. When I tried to explain that my house was haunted, they'd quickly interrupt and insist that rather than my house being haunted, *I* was possessed. Furthermore, they insisted that I was not a born-again Christian, and that I needed to repent of all my sins in front of everyone, and I needed to name each sin.

As I tried to explain that I was already a born-again Christian, they again shushed me and continued with their agenda. It's embarrassing to admit it now, but I was *so* desperate that I went along with their game. There I stood, confessing things to strangers that I'd already settled with God. When that was complete, they started trying to cast demons out of me. When nothing manifested despite their best efforts, Pastor Mark then began trying to force me to speak in tongues. When this also failed, one woman stepped forward and said, "Make sure you're telling us everything," as if confessing more sins would suddenly help me speak in tongues.

Eventually, they gave up and pretended as though they'd ridded me of demons. After the service ended, David, Pastor Mark, and several others promised they'd come to my house and pray with me, at a later date that fit all of their schedules. As I drove home, I felt numb. It was obvious that the church advertised my attendance as a freak show, which would include a live exorcism. Perhaps they thought this so-called exorcism would put their little church on the map and draw in parishioners.

I also couldn't help but notice that David's behavior was markedly different when he was in the presence of his pastor. It was almost like he was a totally different person. Pastor Mark, in my opinion, had no real knowledge of spiritual warfare or exorcism and also had a shaky foundation for his theology. Sooner or later, he and I would butt heads.

As I struggled to find something positive about the experience, I reminded myself that at least they had promised to come to the property and pray with me. I was confident that if other believers would walk the property and pray in agreement with me, I actually had a fighting chance of overcoming the evil that was trying to destroy me. I hoped they would come soon.

## CHAPTER THIRTY-FIVE

### FRIDAY THE 13TH

*A*s the days wore on, the negative emotions of my experience at the church began taking their toll. Feelings of desperation and hopelessness began rearing their ugly heads once again. On the following Friday evening, November 13, 2009, I hit a breaking point. Blinded by all the negativity, it hadn't occurred to me that it was a satanic holiday. This probably had an effect on me, considering the environment in which I lived. As I was driving home from work, I began venting my frustration to God.

"I can't take this anymore. I have asked for help so many times, and this all just drags on. I give up! I don't even care anymore, and I'm not going to believe anymore. If you want to change this situation, that is your business, but I'm not going to believe any longer! I'm done!" I spouted in my haze of frustration and foolishness.

When I arrived home, I entered the house, turned on the lights, and walked through the foyer to the great room, where I disarmed the security system. I then walked back through the foyer, turned and went upstairs to my bedroom, and checked my answering machine. I then exited my bedroom and started back down the stairs into the foyer, when I noticed something that made my blood run cold. Just as on the day when David had first visited, the curtain over the vertical window on the right side of the front door had once again been manipulated!

I descended the stairs and took a closer look, and discovered that again the top section of the curtain had been moved. This time, however, the magnetic curtain rod had been not only turned at a strange angle, but also pulled apart, and the magnet now hung over the wooden strip between the window's steel frame and the steel door. The magnet wasn't even touching the steel of the window frame! Clearly, whatever did this wanted to make it abundantly obvious that this was yet another example of paranormal activity.

Realizing that my statements of unbelief had left me vulnerable to the spirits haunting me, I immediately began repenting for what I'd said to God earlier that evening while driving home.

"God, I'm sorry. *I DO BELIEVE IN YOU!* Please forgive me and protect me. Jesus, I'm sorry!" I prayed as I realized how powerless I was without God. I then began binding the demons in Jesus' name.

One very unsettling detail of this incident is that I completely believe that the curtain had been moved *after* I'd entered the house and gone upstairs to check the answering machine. Otherwise, it would have been virtually impossible to walk through the foyer, facing the door, without noticing something so obvious. In fact, before I'd turned to go upstairs, the curtain would have been directly in front of and very close to me. There's no way I could not have seen this.

Although the moving of this curtain and curtain rod might seem minor to some people, when things in your home are moving by themselves or being manipulated by unseen hands, it can be terrifying! Things like this are *not* supposed to happen. I took several pictures of how the curtain had been manipulated, and a couple of the entire door and window with the strange residue. I then called Mom and told her what happened.

"I'm coming right out, Patrick!" she said when she got the news.

"No, that's ok. I'll be all right. I hate for you to drive all the way out here," I assured her.

"I'm coming out. I'll be there in a little while!" she insisted. To be honest, I wasn't comfortable being in the house alone after what had just transpired, so I welcomed the company. It certainly couldn't hurt having a prayer warrior like Mom there, at least for a little while.

*The curtain rod had been manipulated so that the magnet was now over the wood strip between the door and window.*

*It would have been impossible for the cats to move the curtain rod and not disturb the rest of the curtain.*

Once Mom arrived, I showed her how the curtain rod had been manipulated and then went outside and took some more pictures. Strangely enough, once outside, I began hearing an owl in the thin brush line that separated my property from Eli's.

Finding this peculiar, I went to the brush line and shined a flashlight into the few sparse trees where the noises were coming from, but there was no evidence whatsoever of an owl, other than the noise I was still hearing. As close as I was to where the noises were coming from, I should have easily been able to see the owl, but I couldn't. Furthermore, I'd never experienced an owl that close to my house before.

I couldn't ignore the possible connection between the strange owl sounds on the night I experienced more paranormal activity, and the Native Americans who had allegedly cursed my land. I did some research on what the owl symbolized among the Native American tribes, and learned that it was regarded as a sign of the supernatural, death and witchcraft. I also learned that hearing an owl hooting was believed by the Indians to be a sign of a bad omen. Was this more evidence of an Indian curse on the land?

I did a little more digging and learned that the owl is also a symbol of both Lucifer and witchcraft. I couldn't help but speculate that the elusive owl represented multiple forms of evil that I was facing.

One thing I knew for sure was that there was no room for even momentary unbelief, no matter what my future might hold. The evil I was cohabitating with fed off these negative emotions, and I knew more than ever that I didn't stand a chance without God.

Later, I called David to explain the incident and see how soon he and the others from his church could come to walk the property with me. His answer was disappointing.

"Well, there are several people from church who want to come along, but we have to do it when we can coordinate all of our schedules," he explained.

Again, I imagined the church advertising their visit to my property as a public outing where all were welcome. I simply needed a couple of people to come and help me, but this was beginning to feel more like a social event for entertainment's sake. I tried to hide my disappointment and frustration as I politely thanked David and hung up the phone. For the time being, all I could do was wait.

Later, after I downloaded the pictures from my camera to my computer, I found that when I zoomed in on one of the pictures of the window on the front door, I noticed what looked like several faces on the glass. There was the strange residue that somewhat looked like a face, but then in other parts of the window, I saw more faces. I believe these are merely reflections that just happen to look like faces, but when I showed the pictures to others, they saw them too. I still don't put a lot of stock into these faces, but I do find them interesting, all things considered.

# CHAPTER THIRTY-SIX

## THE DOORKEEPER!

As days turned into weeks, I tried my best to be patient. Thanksgiving came and went and I couldn't even bring myself to celebrate with family. I continually found myself pushing Rebecca away as well, because I knew that barring a miracle, I'd likely lose everything within months.

When I finally received the call I'd been waiting for from David, he informed me that a group from his church could come to the house on Wednesday evening, December 2. I thanked him and held out hope that their visit would finally rid me of the demons that had haunted me mercilessly for the past several years of my life.

When the day finally arrived, it rained steadily much of the afternoon, but I knew walking the property was crucial. That evening, a group consisting of David, Pastor Mark, a middle-aged woman named Carol, and two women in their thirties named Tina and Amanda arrived shortly after dark. Carol was said to have a very keen spiritual gift known as the discerning of spirits, meaning she had the ability to identify demons.

After welcoming the group into my home, I began telling them about the paranormal activity I'd witnessed. Almost immediately, Pastor Mark and David put a stop to that, claiming that I was glorifying evil spirits if I even talked about what they'd done.

"No, I'm not glorifying them. I'm just trying to tell you what I've been dealing with," I responded.

I then explained that I knew we needed to walk the property and pray in order to drive the spirits out. I also explained that I believed anointing the property with anointing oil and taking communion on the land were necessary. I knew from doing deliverance ministry on people that things that are spiritually symbolic, such as communion and anointing oil, are very powerful against demons.

"Well, we're not going to walk the property because it's too wet." David said as he looked down at his shiny white sneakers.

With that, I knew the evening was likely going to be a waste of my time. If even two of them had come weeks earlier, I believed my situation might have already changed. However, since they'd invited everyone to join in on the fun, they'd had to wait until tonight so each person's schedule would allow their participation. They did agree to pray with me in the kitchen, however, so I hoped for the best.

We stood in a basic circle and began praying, when Carol suddenly interjected, "I know what its name is. It's telling me its name. Do you want to know?"

"Yes, I want to know. What's its name?" I asked.

"It calls itself the *Doorkeeper*," she responded.

I'd run into "gatekeeper" demons before during exorcisms, but I wasn't sure if this was the same type of spirit. We prayed a little more, asking for God's help. When we finished praying, I was a little relieved when Carol asked to walk around the house to see what else she might discern. When we went to the basement, she immediately focused on the crack that had kept reappearing in the basement wall under the front door.

"This is significant! This is relevant to what's going on here. Upstairs, what's directly above this crack?" she asked.

"Directly above this is the front door," I answered.

"This is definitely significant," she confidently stated yet again.

I hadn't thought about how that crack might be relevant before Carol's assertion, but I found it interesting that my weight bench had been directly in front of the crack when I had my accident and tore my pectoral muscle in 2006. I thought of how the weight had suddenly felt much heavier than it actually was. I then remembered Chelsea's claim of repeatedly seeing Moses in the basement when he wasn't even there. Perhaps Carol was onto something.

When we returned upstairs, Carol focused on the foyer and slowly walked to the front door again. Standing in front of the door, she moved her hand back and forth between the door and the front living room and staircase.

"I feel something here. There is something in this area. Like something comes and goes through here," she stated confidently. She then looked at the strange residue on the window of the door.

"I feel like this is just a natural anomaly in the glass," she stated.

"But that isn't *in* the glass, Carol. Whatever it is, it's *on* the glass," I replied.

"Well, I wouldn't worry about it, but there *is* something peculiar about the door itself. Like I said, I believe something comes and goes through this doorway," she answered.

Sadly, other than the insight Carol offered, the evening was less than beneficial. Eventually, Pastor Mark forbade her from speaking any further to me. The rest of the night was spent debating moot points of nonsense with Pastor Mark, Tina and Amanda. Pastor Mark jumped from position to position as he went from arguing first that the house wasn't haunted, to later stating that if it was haunted, it was my fault. At one point, while he argued that the house couldn't be haunted because a Christian can't have a haunted house, Pastor Mark made a statement so ignorant that it was all I could do not to escort the group to the door.

"A Christian can't have a haunted house because they have the Holy Spirit. It's like I told my young son the other day when he complained of a sore throat. 'You can't have a sore throat because you have the Holy Spirit.' You can't be sick if you're filled with the Spirit,' I told him," he arrogantly proclaimed.

I was angered not only by the arrogance and ignorance of that statement, but also by how dangerous the false beliefs of much of the church have become regarding spiritual warfare. I tried in vain to explain what I'd learned about the alleged Indian curse on the land, as well as the witchcraft that was being practiced by those living around me. I knew in my heart that if they'd just stop arguing and help me break the curses, I would likely be free. Again, I was baffled by David's strange behavior as well. When he came to the house alone, he believed me and wanted to help, but when in the presence of Pastor Mark, he was like a completely different person.

Tina and Amanda, under the influence of Pastor Mark, then began accusing me of being fascinated by the demonic and enjoying the haunting activity that had plagued me. Tina, who was sitting on the couch with my coffee-table-sized version of the King James Bible open on her lap, suddenly stood up and disrespectfully slammed the Bible shut loudly as she leveled more ridiculous accusations. I was trying to take the high road, but I'd had enough.

"Have you ever cast a demon out of anyone?" I asked.

"Well, no, but what does that have to do with anything?" she arrogantly replied.

"Well, I have. I know what I'm talking about, and I know what I'm doing. All I wanted was for someone to come here and walk the property and pray in agreement with me to drive the demons out!" I reminded them as I finally began venting my frustration.

"Look, there is no 'doorkeeper' here now. The house doesn't feel haunted to *me*. Everything feels peaceful here now to *me*," Pastor Mark interjected in a haughty tone.

"And if there were any demons here, *you* had to have invited them in because *you* built the house," he continued.

"Have you listened to anything I've been trying to tell you? If the land had already been cursed before the house was built, the curse could cause the house to be haunted. Look—never mind. Forget it!" I countered as I saw the futility of trying to argue obvious truths with someone so willingly ignorant.

Sensing that I was likely to call it a night, they then shifted to recruitment mode, trying to lure me to their church. They tried to use guilt to make me subservient to them. Remember, they'd already made me confess all my sins to them publicly, a few weeks earlier at church. Eventually they halfheartedly prayed with me, but still insisted I'd created my own problems.

As if things couldn't get any stranger, Tina then stood and faced me and began marching in place as she "prophesied" over me that she saw me leading worship in a church. As crazy as that incident was, I actually did lead worship occasionally years later at a Nazarene church. Considering, however, that almost everywhere you looked in the house sat a guitar, her so-called "prophesy" would have been a safe one for anyone to make.

Before they left, David reiterated the group's nonsensical view of my situation once again.

"You are *never* to speak of the Doorkeeper ever again. Don't tell anyone. If you even speak of this again, you're only glorifying the devil!" he scolded.

Although I was extremely frustrated, I thanked them for coming, even though I knew my nightmare wasn't over. We hadn't walked the property, taken communion on the land, or anointed anything, and I knew that they hadn't **really** prayed in agreement with me about anything. How could they when our views were polar opposites? At least I did have another clue thanks to Carol identifying the Doorkeeper.

After their departure, I sat alone, digesting and rehashing the evening's events. As I remembered all the paranormal activity over the years involving the front door and foyer area, as well as other doors in the house, I couldn't escape the significance of Carol's claim of the Doorkeeper. I felt very unsettled as more puzzle pieces seemed to fall together in front of me. It was no wonder that I'd had so many experiences of feeling watched, even dating back to the first times I'd stepped foot into the house alone, while it was being built (chapter 2).

Now the evil had a name, and for some reason, this made all the attacks I'd endured seem more personal. Even more disturbing was the name this demon called itself. I'd learned from experience that "gatekeeper" demons had the authoritative function of bringing in more demons and controlling the gate through which they came. I had a sickening feeling then, and I'm even more certain now, that this demon served a similar function and controlled a door or portal through which other demons entered my house and property. Furthermore, if the crack in the basement wall under the front door was as significant as Carol claimed, then this portal that the Doorkeeper controlled came from below the house, or hell itself.

With my thoughts racing, I called Mom and told her this new discovery. Sensing I needed not only to talk but also some company, she hopped in her car and made the journey through three counties to just simply be there. When she arrived, we sat and talked for a while as I vented about the evening's earlier events.

"I know nothing left when they prayed with me. I know it's still here, but now I know its name, and for some reason that freaks me out!" I shared.

Because she lived so far away, Mom decided to sleep on the couch and return home the next morning. When it was finally time for me to retire for the evening, I went to the bathroom at the top of the stairs in the foyer, to get ready for bed. While in the bathroom, I suddenly felt the floor shaking. I tried to convince myself that it was my imagination, but the tremors were too significant for that. When I returned downstairs a few minutes later, Mom was sitting next to the fireplace with a stern expression on her face.

"Do you have one of those springy doorstops in this room? The kind that go *boing* if you flick them?" she asked.

"Yes, there's one right behind this door," I said, pointing at the door to the laundry room. "Why, did Moses or Zoe hit it?"

"No. Neither of the cats were even in the room, but I clearly heard something flick that doorstop!"

"How long ago did that happen?" I asked.

"About five minutes ago," she replied.

"Well, five minutes ago, I was upstairs in the bathroom and felt the floor shaking!" I stated as we both acknowledged that the house was still haunted. This proved that church group's visit had been futile.

I couldn't help but feel disgusted again. Nevertheless, it was time for bed, and I had to try to get some sleep so I could get up and go to work the next day. Before returning upstairs, I made sure all the doors were locked, and I armed the security system. At Mom's request, I left the lights on under the kitchen cupboards, but turned out all the other lights on the first floor.

The next morning, Mom shared that after I'd gone upstairs to bed, she saw a large black shadow move from the foyer into the kitchen and then disappear. The way she described it reminded me exactly of the shadow I'd seen twice previously in the same basic area (chapters 8, 13).

Although I was gaining more knowledge of what was haunting my house, I still felt trapped and somewhat hopeless. Two days later on Friday, December 4, I was off work, so I decided to see if I could get any results by again walking the property alone. This time, however, I had some new clues. I took some grape juice, wafers, and a bottle of anointing oil and headed to the field behind the house. There I began by taking communion and praying, breaking the curses over the land, and telling the demons to leave. I then walked the entire property, anointing the corners with oil. I took my time and tried to be thorough, but I knew that doing this alone wasn't going to be as powerful as if I had other Christians praying with me.

When I finished and returned to the house, I checked my cell phone and saw that I'd missed a phone call from David. I called him back and found what he told me peculiar.

"Patrick, when I left your house the other night and started up the road, I felt like the Lord said to me, 'You should have taken communion with him.' I'm sorry I didn't, and if you want me to, I'll come out and do it as soon as I can," he said.

"David, I appreciate your offer, but I actually was out back taking communion on the land by myself when you called," I answered.

We both found the timing of his call very interesting, and I took it as a sign that, as I suspected, taking communion on the land was important. I decided to wait and see if my efforts that day were successful before calling him to come to the property once again. I really did appreciate his offer and couldn't help but notice how once again, David seemed like a completely different person when he was away from the influence of Pastor Mark.

I especially found it ironic that as soon as David was out of Pastor Mark's presence, almost immediately after leaving my house, he felt that God told him he should have done what I knew was a necessary part of my deliverance. We can never underestimate the importance of the biblical wisdom and knowledge of those we choose as our pastors. Their spirituality will have a direct impact on not only our lives, but also our relationship with God. If our pastors have little knowledge of spiritual warfare, we will be hindered in that area.

That evening around 7:00 p.m., as I was standing in my kitchen, I suddenly heard what sounded like a group of women screaming and crying loudly just outside my house. My first thought was that Eli must have had an accident in his sawmill, and Anna Mae was coming for help. As crazy as that seems now, at the time I could think of no other reason why any woman would be in my yard screaming. I immediately ran outside to the yard, and to my surprise, other than Maggie now barking, everything was very quiet and still. I looked all around but could find no explanation for what I'd heard.

"I heard it too, Maggie," I called out to the kennel as I returned to the house. The experience was chilling, and I felt strongly that it validated my suspicion that Indians had murdered white settlers on the land many years earlier. The screams were so loud and terrifying that it was as if women were watching their husbands being murdered before their eyes.

I don't believe in human spirits being the source of paranormal activity, but I do believe demons can mimic humans and horrific events that open doors giving them "legal rights" to infest a house or property and cause it to be haunted.

This experience clearly showed me that my efforts alone that day weren't enough to drive out the evil possessing my property. I knew I was on the right track, but I was going to need help. There is strength in numbers, and the Bible is very clear about that. Two or more Christians praying in agreement are exponentially more powerful than the prayers of a solitary believer (Leviticus 26:8; Deuteronomy 32:30; Matthew 18:19).

Jesus Christ said that where two or three are gathered together in His name, he is in the midst of them (Matthew 18:20). I believed that this scripture alone supported my belief that I needed multiple Christians to gather together in Jesus' name and walk the property and drive the demons out. According to this scripture, if we did this, essentially He would walk with us.

Previously, when David and his friends and pastor came to

the property, they had their own agenda and false doctrine that hindered the prayers. I also knew beyond any shadow of doubt that they hadn't agreed in prayer with me. Their arguments proved that. For my situation to change, it was going to take humble Christians without false agendas, who were sincere in their prayers.

To this day I still don't know why, but I felt strongly that these believers had to be from outside my family. Certainly, Mom, Lory and Matt would have joined me in a heartbeat, but I felt led back to Dennis and Angie. They had come through with crucial information about the history of the land, and I felt strongly that I was supposed to ask for their assistance. I called them and explained what had happened when the group from David's church came, and also what had transpired after I'd walked the property alone the following Friday. After hearing this, they readily agreed to come to the property and help. The best time that fit all of our schedules was Tuesday, December 15, 2009, which was over a week away. I was hopeful that if I could wait, something good might finally happen. I could clearly see that Dennis and Angie were humble and expected nothing for their assistance. They simply saw that a Christian brother was in dire need of their help, and they wanted to be faithful to what they felt God wanted them to do.

Meanwhile on Tuesday, December 8, I was once again teaching guitar lessons to Doc, Sarah and Becky. As always, we congregated in my front living room, which I had converted to a guitar showroom. About halfway through the lesson, as I was strumming the chords of a song I was teaching them, I heard a loud noise but didn't recognize what it was. I continued strumming and noticed Sarah and Becky giving me a strange look.

"What?" I asked.

"Aren't you going to get that?" they both replied.

"Get what?" I asked, totally oblivious to what they were talking about.

"The door. Someone just rang your doorbell," they answered.

"Yeah, I'll get it. I didn't realize that was what I heard because I was strumming the guitar," I answered as I set my guitar down and rushed to the front door.

When I opened the door, no one was there. I stepped out on the porch and looked all around, but still I saw no one. I returned to the front living room, dumbfounded.

"No one was there. Are you sure that's what you heard?" I asked.

"Yes. Someone rang your doorbell," Sarah answered as Doc and Becky agreed.

"I told you before that I have weird things happen out here," I answered.

I then shared more of my strange experiences, and about the group coming from the church, and what Carol had shared about the Doorkeeper. As we discussed the situation, I then told them about the odd faces in the window in one of the pictures I'd taken after the curtain had moved. Doc and Becky chuckled a bit, but Sarah again affirmed that she believed me because she'd also had paranormal experiences in the past.

A couple of days later, Doc contacted me and ask that I send him the picture of the faces on the door so he could take a look and then forward it to Sarah, who also wanted to see it. I obliged and emailed him the picture. The next day, Sarah contacted me and said she'd had a very strange experience when Doc forwarded the picture to her.

"Patrick, I asked Doc to forward the picture to me so I could see it too. He did, and when I opened the email and tried to view the picture, my computer screen suddenly turned to nothing but static, like an old black-and-white television set. I've never seen a computer screen do that before!"

I had never seen a computer screen do that before either, and until now I'd never heard of such a thing. I now believe that this strange incident was more related to the picture being of the door itself than the strange residue or reflected faces on the glass. If the door was a type of portal for demonic spirits, that would certainly explain why Sarah, who'd had paranormal experiences in the past, might have a reaction when trying to view the picture. When thinking on these things, Tuesday, December 15, couldn't arrive soon enough.

*When Sarah tried to view this picture on her computer, the monitor screen turned to static, like an old black-and-white television set.*

## CHAPTER THIRTY-SEVEN

### DRIVING OUT DEVILS

When Tuesday, December 15 finally arrived, it was a cold cloudy day. I knew in my heart that this might be my last chance, and if it didn't work, I was basically finished. My life felt like a living hell already, but I knew it could get worse. After waking, I showered, made coffee, and waited for Dennis and Angie to arrive. They called and said they were running a little late, but they'd be there soon. After their arrival, they mentioned that they'd had some family issues, but downplayed them. I could tell by glances they shot each other, however, that they'd already overcome significant obstacles just to be there. Part of me wrestled with guilt for what they might be suffering for helping me. I knew full well that the devil doesn't just lie down and take it when it comes time to do battle.

Dennis and Angie were both quiet and humble as we discussed my situation while walking throughout the house. They listened intently, and when they spoke, I felt like I could trust what they were saying.

"Pat, I have to tell you that when we crossed the bridge (over Crabapple Creek) and pulled into your drive, I did get an uneasy feeling. I can't really explain it, but it was very strange. Your house looked so nice, yet I felt uncomfortable, like something wasn't right here," Angie explained.

Dennis then offered help with the problems I'd endured from my Amish neighbors. "Pat, I also want you to know that if you want me to, I'll go around to the Amish out here and talk to them for you. I know a lot of them, and I speak Dutch. I'll tell them you're a good guy, and they'd better leave you alone."

"Dennis, I hope it doesn't come to that, but if this doesn't work today, I may take you up on your offer," I replied.

I'd developed a plan of attack based on many scriptures, my own experience with exorcism, and also the teachings of Bob Larson, Perry Stone, Derek Prince, and a few other deliverance ministers. I knew if this was going to work, I needed to be thorough. I explained to Dennis and Angie that I felt strongly that as part of the exorcism, we should not only anoint the entire property with oil, but also take communion with the land. I really had no idea if the Indians had merely used a word curse on the land, or if they'd also used objects as part of the curse. If they'd used objects such as arrowheads, which they shot into the ground to symbolize the curse, it might be harder to break. Regardless of what all was behind the curse, I knew this battle would only be won through the power of the blood of Jesus Christ. Nothing could stand against that, no matter how vile or demonic.

The time came to begin the exorcism. We weren't priests or preachers, but rather three ordinary people who believed in Jesus Christ. Some might say that we couldn't possibly combat something so evil, but we believed with God's help, we were more than conquerors (Romans 8:37).

We took our anointing oil, grape juice, and wafers and headed toward the field behind my house. When we reached the large hickory tree that served as the border between my backyard and field, we stopped and began preparing for the exorcism. The cold wind whipped against us as we readied ourselves, and as I looked at Dennis and Angie all bundled up, I was taken aback by their humbleness. Certainly the group from David's church would never have braved these cold winds to help me.

"Patrick, however you want to go about this and whatever you want to do, we're in agreement with you," Dennis said, looking me straight in the eyes.

"Thanks, brother, that's what it's going to take," I responded.

I knew I was going to take the shotgun approach and try everything I could think of to break the power of the devil's grip on this land. Because I didn't know 100% exactly what all curses I was dealing with, I was going to be specific in going after *everything* I suspected might be causing the haunting.

We began with prayer, asking God to be merciful and send His Holy Spirit to empower us. We then opened up the grape juice and wafers and took communion, in remembrance of Jesus' sacrifice for our sins. I then laid wafers on the ground and poured grape juice out into the field.

"This represents the body and blood of the Lord Jesus Christ," I began. "Nothing evil can stand against the blood of Jesus. Whatever curses are on the land, we come against you with the blood of Christ, and this juice represents that blood. In the name of Jesus, as the owner of this land, I renounce all sins that have ever happened on this property. I renounce all of my sins and the sins of those before me. I break all curses from those sins in Jesus' name, and I bind all of the demons and command you to leave. I renounce the Doorkeeper in Jesus' name! I renounce all curses from the Greenville Treaty. I renounce all Indian curses on this land, whether they're word curses or cursed objects. I renounce all murder. I renounce all pagan worship of false gods. I renounce all Indian witchcraft. I renounce all Amish witchcraft and curses done against me by those living around me. I renounce powwow practiced by the Amish. I renounce all Satanism practiced in this area. In Jesus' name, I renounce every form of evil that is on this property. I break *all curses* on this land and *all curses that are against me*!" I hesitated for a few moments and then continued.

"We are three Christians praying in agreement against you, which means according to scripture, Jesus is in our midst. I bind all demon spirits and command you to leave, in the name of Jesus Christ. I will not take no for an answer! We command you to leave!"

Dennis and Angie prayed out loud in agreement with me the entire time. We then took the anointing oil and began walking the property while praying and commanding the demons to leave. We anointed all corners of the property and everything we felt led by the Holy Spirit to anoint. After covering the property, we directed our attention to the house itself.

We anointed the front door and again bound the Doorkeeper and commanded him to leave. We then went throughout the house, anointing everything with oil and demanding that all evil spirits leave. We asked for the Holy Ghost to manifest His presence in the house and on the property. Nothing paranormal or supernatural happened while we performed the exorcism, but the house did feel more peaceful when we were finished.

We then sat together in the front living room, and I got my guitar and we sang some worship songs together. Something did seem to be different. After visiting a little longer, Dennis and Angie headed back home, because I had guitar lessons to teach that evening. I sincerely thanked them for coming and helping me, but I knew words alone could not express just how thankful I really was.

That evening, after I taught Doc, Sarah and Becky guitar lessons, I shared with them what had transpired earlier that day. Sarah later contacted me and told me that something very strange had happened to her while she was alone in her car after they'd left my house.

"While I was driving home, my cell phone would ring and light up, but when I'd go to answer it, there was no number or anything showing who was calling. The third time this happened, I answered it and could hear a creepy voice talking, but I couldn't make out what it was saying. It was all garbled and unintelligible. It was very strange, especially after what you'd just told us about the exorcism," she explained.

The following day, Dennis and Angie called and explained that they'd also had strange experiences later that evening.

"After we left your house, I had this overwhelming feeling that we were going to be in an accident and roll the truck. I could even see it happening, and I couldn't shake the feeling. Later on after dark, we were driving, and I thought I saw a bear run out in front of our car, but Angie didn't see anything! Why would I see a bear? It's so rare for any bear to be in Ohio! After that, I was unloading groceries from the back of Deanna's (Angie's daughter) Explorer, when the rear hatch suddenly shut on my hand! There was no explanation for it!" Dennis recounted in a shaky voice.

I apologized for anything that happened because they'd helped me. It was clear that their experiences further validated my claims that the house was haunted, but I felt horrible that they were likely now being oppressed. I was grateful, however, that they'd been willing to put themselves in harm's way to help me. I couldn't help but wonder why the activity seemed to be only directed at Dennis and not Angie. I also found it interesting that these experiences happened to Sarah and Dennis long after they'd left my property, and not while they were there. Was this an indication that the exorcism had worked, and my property was free of evil spirits? For now I'd have to wait and see. As the old saying goes, the proof is in the pudding. If the exorcism was successful, my circumstances would likely change in the near future.

# CHAPTER THIRTY-EIGHT

## THE REVEAL

Christmas time came and went, and for the first time in years, I enjoyed company as I celebrated with Rebecca. I didn't know what my future might hold, but the house felt different, and I had hope again. I no longer had any paranormal experiences in the house, but I still needed the property to sell, and winter wasn't the best season for that. After New Year's, I determined that come what may, I was going to start attending the small Nazarene church that I'd attended a few times in the past. On those previous occasions, however, I'd felt overwhelmingly oppressed when even driving to the church, which made attendance very difficult (chapter 18).

On Sunday, January 3, 2010, I decided I was going to attend an evening Bible study at the church. I got ready and grabbed my Bible, but before I could even back my vehicle down the driveway, my cell phone rang. It was Jill.

"Patrick, I just got a call from a couple who want to come and look at your house. They've driven by several times already. Pat, they're very interested," she said with hope in her voice.

"Wow, that's good news," I said, trying not to get my hopes up.

"So far they've only expressed interest in the house and two acres, but they want to come view it as soon as possible. I will set everything up and get back to you," Jill assured me before hanging up.

Something felt different this time. Could this be the family who'd actually buy the house? Sure, I'd rather sell the entire property than just the house and two acres, but somehow I was able to leave it all in God's hands this time. That night at the Bible study, after I shared the news and requested prayer that the house would finally sell, several other Christians agreed in prayer with me.

Over the next several days, Rebecca and Mom helped me get the house ready to show to the potential buyers. As I was cleaning, I went to the front door with a paper towel and a little Windex and easily washed the strange residue off of the window. It removed so easily that I don't think it could have been sticker residue, as I had tried to convince myself when I'd first noticed it. It has been suggested to me since that time that the residue might have been ectoplasm, which is a peculiar substance often found in haunted houses.

When the day came for the potential buyers to look at the house, I did my best to hide my nervousness. They were a newer order Mennonite family, consisting of a husband and wife in their fifties and two teenage daughters. During the viewing, several people from their church also arrived and went through the house with them.

While standing on the front porch, as I was showing the father the outside of the house, he pointed to a cross in anointing oil that was still on the front door. "What's that all about?" he asked suspiciously.

"Well, I really wanted the house to sell, so a couple of friends and I prayed over the entire house and property and blessed it," I answered.

"Oh, ok," he replied as he chuckled to himself.

My answer was true, but there was no sense in going into

detail about the house being haunted and risking these people thinking I was crazy. Besides, I believed the house was no longer haunted and the blessing had been successful, or they wouldn't even be there talking to me.

After the showing, Jill assured me that the family was very interested. A few days later, they inquired about the remaining acreage. Over the next couple of weeks, we settled on a price, and they agreed to buy the entire property along with the house. The final selling price afforded me the large amount of equity I knew the property possessed. They were, however, ruthless in their demands, and I was left with very little time to find another home and get ready to move.

One day as Jill and I were going over paperwork that needed my signature, she uncovered the original price that Myron and Sarah Jane Miller had paid for the acreage. The Millers had claimed that when they sold the land to us for around $10,500 per acre, they were selling it for *less* than they'd paid (chapter 1). In reality, they'd actually paid less than $4,000 per acre. I struggled to remember any dealing I'd ever had with the Amish in which they'd been honest, but I couldn't think of any. I had to laugh, however, when I remembered how Chelsea had been so proud of herself for negotiating with them, without me being present, and believed she'd gotten such a great price on the land.

As inspectors came during the selling process, I began hearing even more horror stories about the Amish and their control of Holmes County. One inspector named Tom had some very interesting claims, and he didn't try to hide his disdain for the Amish religion. His stories would have been unbelievable had it not been for what I'd witnessed over the last several years.

"My friend has a van and makes money driving the Amish around, because they are forbidden to drive cars. This friend told me that Amish men pay him to drive them to prostitution houses in Massillon, and he has to wait on them while they're inside with the prostitutes," Tom said in disgust. He shook his head and continued.

"I know of an Amish family who has adopted three babies, and all of them have died strange deaths, which they claim are crib death. I'm certain they're killing the babies, but the authorities don't even investigate. Instead, they just keep letting the family adopt more children!" he added.

These stories reinforced what I'd discovered about the corruption in Holmes County and the strong control the Amish religion had over the local government. I couldn't wait to move.

On February 5, 2010, we closed on the sale. As I scrambled to find another house, Rebecca directed me to a large, two-story, all-brick house in a small town in Tuscarawas County. It was built in 1924, but it had recently been remodeled and appeared to be very nice. It sat on the corner of an alley, on the second block of Fifth Street, which seemed like a quiet neighborhood. I didn't have much time to think, so I jumped in with both feet. I just wanted out of Holmes County as soon as possible.

Over several days during the last week of February, with help from relatives and friends, I moved from Holmes County to the new home Rebecca had led me to. It was a bittersweet time, as I couldn't help but remember what I'd dreamed my life would be like when Chelsea and I had bought the land and built the house eight years earlier. Since that time, I'd learned that virtually everything I believed in, other than my faith in God, had proven to be a lie. As I went throughout the house, I was no longer haunted by demonic entities, but now, during those final moments in the house, I was haunted by memories of a beautiful wife, who I'd once foolishly believed loved me, and a home that I'd once thought was a blessing.

On the day I loaded Maggie and Copper into my SUV, I realized that through the hell I'd survived, there had been blessings along the way. If I'd never lived there, I'd never have found Maggie or Copper. I needed them, and they needed me, and I believed that God had brought us together. During my last couple of days of moving, the winter weather was brutal, but we pushed on through the cold and snow as I anticipated what I hoped would be a peaceful new beginning at 220 Fifth Street.

Over the next several months, as I realized a completely new barrage of unexpected activity at my new home, there were a couple of incidents related to my former house, which completely validated my claims of the evil lurking under the surface of the Amish and Mennonite religions. The first incident occurred when I received a phone call from the Census Bureau, in which I was accused of attempting to avoid registering. According to the Census Bureau, the buyers of my property lied and claimed that I'd lived in my former house until the beginning of May 2010. Apparently **they** didn't want to register with the Census, so they claimed to have lived at their former residence until much later in the year.

I explained that this supposedly *"Christian"* family had lied to them. I then referred the Census Bureau worker to my Realtor for proof of when I'd moved out of the residence. This was, once again, another example of Amish and Mennonites passing themselves off as holy and humble, while they saw nothing wrong with lying about me and potentially causing me legal problems with the government.

As if that wasn't annoying enough, the second incident was more insidious. In April, I along with Lory and Matt returned to the property in Holmes County to get a sign I'd used for my guitar store. When we came down the township road that led to my former property, as we neared the location where a bull steer skull had been hanged from a tree one year earlier, I saw another peculiar sight. I stopped my vehicle, got out, and went closer for a better look. To my horror, I found a dead dog hanging from a tree by its foot. Once again, I felt the fury of the last several years rising in me. This was a clear and undeniable sign that, just as I had long suspected, someone near me was practicing Satanism.

Because this was Amish-owned land and was in plain sight from Eli's house, I had to conclude that the culprits were Amish. I took pictures, called the sheriff, and reported the incident. The three of us were completely sickened by this blatant symbol of evil in a county that so profited from a false image of "Christianity."

This was also the exact same location where Chelsea had found Copper nearly eight years earlier. Could it be that the devil worship in that location might have been the *real* reason why Copper sat there for hours on end, as if he was afraid to move (chapter 3)? Because animals can often sense things that humans cannot, this is certainly a reasonable suspicion.

I then remembered that I'd also seen a raccoon in that exact location, sitting in the middle of the road, shaking. I'd even beeped the horn, and it still wouldn't move, as if it was too scared to do anything. Also, Lory had reported seeing a groundhog in the exact same location, exhibiting identical behavior. After finding the dog, I had no choice but to conclude that all of these incidents are related.

I've shown pictures of the dog to police from areas outside Holmes County, as well as paranormal investigators, and they all agree that this is a sign of Satanism. I realize that my claims of an Indian curse on the land and Amish neighbors practicing witchcraft and Satanism will come under scrutiny, but this latest find is very difficult to dispute. Someone near my property was undoubtedly heavily into the occult. Ultimately, I believe God allowed me to find that dog so I'd have more concrete proof of my claims of what was being practiced in the Amish community.

Ironically, when I later obtained the sheriff's department report for my call about this dog, I discovered that as usual, the deputy had downplayed the incident and simply claimed that the dog appeared to have been hit by a vehicle. He neglected to mention the oddity of the dog hanging from a tree by its foot, or that this clearly is a sign of Satanism. As usual, because the Amish reputation must be protected, the incident was swept under the rug. Considering the millions of tourist dollars that the Amish draw to Holmes County annually, it's no wonder. This is just as the Bible says, "The love of money is the root of all evil" (1 Timothy 6:10).

I believe the events of December, January and February reveal substantial evidence that the exorcism was indeed successful. The house and property had been on the market for nearly three years already, yet within eighteen days of the exorcism, the buyers expressed serious interest, and within fifty-one days we closed on the sale. Furthermore, the paranormal activity ceased after the exorcism. After my experiences, it is impossible for me to believe that the timing of these events was coincidental. I instead choose to believe that a merciful God intervened at the time that He ordained, and delivered me from my nightmare.

*This dead dog hanging from a tree on Amish property near my house was undeniable proof of Satanism and witchcraft in Amish country.*

# CHAPTER THIRTY-NINE

## THE WRAP

*B*ecause the details of my deliverance are supported by biblical principles, it would be improper to witness such a dynamic move of God and not share my testimony with others. As the world around us becomes more evil seemingly by the day, paranormal activity and demonization are on the rise almost exponentially. Therefore, the church needs to understand spiritual warfare like never before.

Sadly, however, it seems the church is growing more and more ignorant in this important area. There are also many misconceptions about what causes a house to be haunted, and most Christians believe that hauntings are the homeowner's fault. They believe that *you* must have opened doors to evil spirits if your house is haunted. The fact of the matter is that while people can cause their own problems, more often than not, houses are haunted because of something that defiled the house or property and brought a curse, often many years earlier. Until someone comes along and deals with the curse and makes the demons leave, it will remain haunted regardless of who lives there.

Another misconception was demonstrated by Pastor Mark

(chapter 36), who claimed that a Christian cannot have a haunted house because they have the Holy Spirit. This only brings condemnation on the person who is already suffering oppression. Not only is this unbiblical, but history disproves this view as well. For instance, according to an article published in *Arminian* magazine, from December 2, 1716, to the end of January 1717, Reverend Samuel Wesley, the father of great theologians John and Charles Wesley, suffered severe paranormal activity in the family home in Lincolnshire.

Mr. Wesley was not only a devout Christian, but also a clergyman in the Church of England. The haunting was so severe that other clergymen advised him to flee the house. To that Mr. Wesley responded, "No; Let the Devil flee from me. I will never flee from the Devil."

As stated, I believe that multiple biblical principles came into play, which resulted in my deliverance. Many steps led to the day of the exorcism on the house and land, and each was significant. One of the most important was a lifestyle of repentance. Although I blew it spiritually many times while going through my nightmare, I always repented and kept trying. Without this repentance I would have spiraled out of control spiritually, and legal rights would have been given to the demons to torment me to even greater levels.

Prayer throughout the time I experienced the haunting was also critical. God only knows what might have befallen me without divine intervention because of my prayers and the prayers of others. Prayer was not only an integral part of survival, but also the exorcism itself. Also, the power of Christians praying in agreement cannot be overstated. The power of praying grows exponentially when born-again believers agree in their prayers (Matthew 18:19–20).

Fasting played a critical role in my deliverance as well, as I believe it brought about a series of events in the spiritual realm, which led me down the path to deliverance. Shortly after fasting in September, other significant opportunities presented themselves. In addition, fasting can weaken the power of specific demons and also increase our faith. It is impossible to cast out certain types of demons without fasting (Mark 9:29).

My step of faith in pledging a $1000 seed into Inspiration Ministries undoubtedly also brought about untold blessings in my life (chapter 30). For instance, Mike Murdock had stated that he believed that those who pledged a $1,000 seed would receive the following:

1. Favor with people who could change your situation.
2. A hundredfold return on your seed.
3. Ideas that would change your situation.

Each of those claims proved to be true. Almost immediately after taking that step of faith, I came into contact with Angie and Dennis, who not only held the secret of the curse on the land, but also stood in faith with me during the exorcism. They had no pretenses or hidden motives, and just wanted to be faithful and help someone in need. Ironically, I do believe that having favor with Carol was also important because she identified the Doorkeeper. This helped me be more specific in some regards during the exorcism.

Through the equity in the house when it sold, and tax breaks and incentives, I did receive a hundredfold return on the $1,000 seed I pledged to Inspiration Ministries. One reason this gift was critical is because I believe God wanted me to boldly step out in faith financially, knowing he would bless my faith, according to the scriptures.

*Malachi 4:10,11: Bring ye all the tithes into the storehouse, that there may be meat in mine house, and prove me now herewith, saith the Lord of hosts, if I will not open you the windows of heaven, and pour you out a blessing, that there shall not be room enough to receive it. And I will rebuke the devourer for your sakes, and he shall not destroy the fruits of your ground; neither shall your vine cast her fruit before the time in the field, saith the Lord of hosts.*

\* \* \*

WRITING about my experiences is certainly an idea that has changed my circumstances. Through what I've endured, I've learned how to help others who, like me, feel trapped in a never-ending nightmare. It is humbling and invigorating to help someone else overcome the enemy of their soul, through the power of Jesus Christ. I'm now able to help others who are oppressed or possessed. My circumstances have certainly changed.

Sadly, there was a tangible reason why Dennis seemed to be heavily oppressed after the exorcism. Unknown at the time was the fact that Dennis had dark secrets from his time spent in the Amish community, and these secrets left him vulnerable. While living with the Amish, Dennis had suffered some of the worst forms of abuse imaginable. Now, as an adult, he managed to hide the fact that he carried the burden of the typical issues that accompany those forms of abuse. Although I know Dennis was sincere in the help he offered me, because of the abuse he'd suffered at the hands of the Amish, he was in need of deliverance himself. A few years after they'd stood beside me, fighting the invisible war, Dennis and Angie divorced because of his marital infidelity. Before their divorce, I sat down with Dennis and urged him to seek spiritual deliverance before making any major decisions. I even offered an exorcism. Sadly, even though he acknowledged he has demons, he refused the offer and went ahead with the divorce. This unfortunate situation demonstrated the fruit of a religious cult that hides great wickedness behind false holiness and humility. Although Dennis made his decisions of his own free will, all too often, abuse victims struggle in ways others can't even imagine. Regardless of Dennis' actions after they helped me, I will always be grateful for his help, and my offer for exorcism still stands.

In the years that have passed since I moved from Holmes County, I have uncovered more evidence that witchcraft and Satanism are alive and well among the Amish. I've discovered multiple satanic meeting sites, in addition to the one located near my former home. I've visited some of these sites and gathered photo and video evidence as well.

While doing more research about the history of the area, I contacted a local historical society. Although the gentleman I spoke with knew less about the history of my land than I did, he did share two disturbing pieces of information. After I mentioned my paranormal experiences and explained where my former property was located, the man stated that he was aware of someone living not far from me, who had killed and skinned a rabbit in a witchcraft ritualistic sacrifice. He then added that a retired doctor, who also lived not far from my former house, had uncovered human remains buried on his property, while a gas pipeline was being installed. The retired doctor allegedly just covered up the bones and didn't report his findings to the authorities.

I've also obtained several books that further validate my claims of secret occult activity practiced by the Amish. One such book is **HEX**, a former best seller by Arthur H. Lewis, which details a true story of murder and witchcraft among the Amish. In his book, Lewis documents how the Amish practice various forms of witchcraft such as pow-wow, and witchcraft from ancient occult books known as the **Sixth and Seventh Books of Moses**. As part of my research, I also obtained the Amish witch-craft book **POW-WOWS or Long Lost Friend** written by John George Hohman, as well as the **Sixth and Seventh Books of Moses**.

After examining these books, it was obvious why I'd been under so much oppression, if those around me were using these writings to place hexes and conjure demons. That, coupled with curses on my land from the Native Americans, created the perfect storm of demonic oppression. During my struggles, however, I learned that just like when the disciples found themselves in a great storm on the Sea of Galilee, Jesus is able to calm any storm (Matthew 8:23–27; Mark 4:36–41). It is our responsibility to keep the faith and apply biblical principles when these storms arise.

So, dear reader, you've now heard my story firsthand. Whether you're reading my testimony for entertainment's sake, or looking for deliverance from your own nightmare, I can assure you it is true. It's not my intention to glorify the powers of the kingdom of darkness, but rather to share hope that can only be found in the name of Jesus. The Bible is true, my friend. There is a God, and there is a Devil. Heaven and Hell are real, as are angels and demons. As an unseen war rages all around us, we each must choose to either fight the good fight of faith, or to follow the easy road that leads to destruction. What you choose is up to you. I choose to fight!

**\* \* \***

This is where the first edition of
NIGHTMARE IN HOLMES COUNTY
ended. The following is additional content added for the second edition. This content serves to further prove the claims of haunting, occult activity, and Satanism in what is perhaps the largest population of Amish in the world.

# CHAPTER FORTY

## HOLMES COUNTY REVISITED 2020

S ince *Nightmare in Holmes County* was first published in February 2015, several movies have documented witchcraft among the Amish. These movies include the 2016 Lifetime Channel's *Amish Witches – The True Story of Holmes County*, and *The Harvesting*, which was also released in 2016. In my research for *Nightmare in Holmes County*, I uncovered much more evidence that proved that Holmes County is a hotbed for the occult and haunting activity. I will now share this evidence.

\* \* \*

In 2011 I contacted a friend and web designer, Christian Ervin, to build a website for the release of my first book, *220 Fifth Street*. As I was working with Christian, we often discussed the paranormal. As I shared some of my experiences regarding Holmes County, Christian told me a story that shook even me to my core.

"Pat, I know that there is a lot of witchcraft among the Amish because I've seen it. I have a story to tell you that you won't believe, and I have a picture that will blow your mind."

"Ok, go ahead," I said with anticipation.

"Well, a few years ago my brother and some friends took me to a couple of places in Holmes County that they claim are haunted. One is called Panther Hollow. They told me that Satanism and witchcraft are practiced there. The other place is an old grave yard called 'the Headless Angel.'

"We went to the Headless Angel first. It's an old cemetery way out in the country in Holmes County. There is a huge angel statue there, and it's missing its head. People go there and mess with the statue, and then bad things happen to them. Like…I know this guy who urinated on it. The next day he couldn't pee, and he believed it was because of what he had done to the angel statue. I'm telling you, the place is creepy."

Christian hesitated and then continued. "But then things got even weirder. We went to Panther Hollow. It's a lonely road through a valley surrounded by Amish farms. There was an old shed there where people practiced witchcraft and Satanism. If you go inside, there are parts of animals lying around from sacrifices, and there are pentagrams painted on the walls. Throughout the whole valley there are satanic things painted on all the trees. As if that isn't bad enough…it gets worse. We happened to be there on a night when there was a satanic meeting happening, off in a field that we could see from the road. We could see a burning pentagram and people in black standing around it. My brother started taking pictures. After taking a few, we then figured it was time to go. As we were driving home, our group was in two cars. I was in one car, and my brother was in the other. He called me on my cell phone and told me to pull over because he had something to show me. We pulled both cars to the edge of the road, and my brother got out. He quickly approached me with his camera and said, 'Look at this picture, Christian! This is the picture I took of the burning pentagram with the people in black. There is nothing there, and the picture is all black. How can the pentagram and people not be in the picture? But then I noticed something on the side that looked lighter…like something *was* there. I lightened the picture, and look at what you can see!'

"My brother handed me the camera. I looked at it and couldn't believe what I saw. Where there should have been a picture of a burning pentagram, I saw a face staring back at me. You can see through the face, like it's a spirit. We saw nothing like that when he took the picture! There is no explanation for the face, or for why the pentagram and people are not in the picture!"

Christian then proceeded to give me a copy of the picture. Just as he said, there is a face looking back into the camera. The face is distorted and you can see through it, but it is clearly there.

"And regardless of what others may tell you, the people doing the ritual were Amish. It was happening on their land, and it was the Amish doing it!" Christian added.

Christian then made me an offer that was hard to refuse.

"If you ever want to go there, I'll take you!"

*Where there should have been a burning pentagram and cult members, the picture instead shows an eerie face.*

After viewing the picture and hearing Christian's account of

207

supernatural events at Panther Hollow, I took him up on his offer. Shortly thereafter I accompanied him to both the Headless Angel cemetery, and Panther Hollow. We drove the twisting, turning lonely roads of Holmes County until we reached the cemetery, located just off Township Road 110. The cemetery's actual name is the Salem Cemetery, but it was immediately clear why it had been nicknamed the Headless Angel. Inside the gates stood a gravestone that served as a pedestal for a tall statue that overshadowed all the other grave markers. The statue was an angel that was missing its head, hands, and wings, from years of vandalism and harsh weather. The cemetery certainly had an eerie feel, but I wondered if there was any way to validate the claims of haunting, or the alleged supernatural powers of the statue. For now it was time to move on to our next stop— Panther Hollow.

We left the cemetery and drove a short distance to a forbidding, small road that cut through a valley surrounded by Amish farms. This was it, we were in Panther Hollow. As we drove deeper into the valley, I began seeing satanic symbols painted on trees. On one tree were the words "the devil will rise," and on another the numbers "666." It seemed that everywhere I looked there was evidence of satanic worship. The word *DEATH* was written backwards on another tree. I knew this was significant, because the most notorious satanist of the twentieth century, Aleister Crowley, had taught his students to write words backwards. What went on at Panther Hollow was the real deal. These were real, dyed-in-the-wool satanists.

Christian slowed his truck to a halt. "Look over there. See that clearing and that field in the distance?" he asked.

"Yeah, I see it," I answered.

"That is where the burning pentagram and cult members were. This is where we were standing when that picture was taken," he said.

*The headless angel towers over all the other graves, dominating the landscape.*

REPLICA OF ORIGINAL ANGEL

*A rendition of the angel before the elements and vandals took its head, hands and wings.*

Christian then drove forward, further into the valley. A short distance later he stopped the truck again. "See that pile right there?" he asked while motioning towards a pile of burnt wood and brush.

"Yeah, I see it…What is it?" I replied.

"That pile of rubble is what is left of that shed where they did satanic animal sacrifices. Someone burned it down," he answered.

I got out of the truck and left the road. I had to get closer to inspect the debris. I found a pile of charred wood that was beginning to be grown over by brush. I was standing on top of what was left of the shed where animals had been sacrificed to Satan. I then remembered seeing the word "Die" with a five-letter expletive painted on a tree. I couldn't help but wonder if it was only animals that were sacrificed. With all the incest and undocumented births among the Amish, if a human sacrifice had occurred, no one would know.

Something else I noticed while in Panther Hollow was a strange noise that sounded like a men's choir holding one note perpetually. I couldn't tell what direction the sound was emanating from, as it seemed to come from all directions at once.

As we left the hollow and returned home, I felt a familiar, uneasy feeling that I had often experienced while living in Holmes County. The more I thought about it, I felt compelled to once again pray warfare prayers over myself, my house, and my property.

# CHAPTER FORTY-ONE

## HALLOWEEN 2012

*I*n 2012 I was promoting my book *220 Fifth Street* full time. I was offered a weekly spot on Blogtalk radio as part of the Kapow Radio Network. I accepted and began recording weekly shows dealing with spiritual warfare and the paranormal. I decided that on Halloween 2012, I would broadcast live from the Headless Angel cemetery and Panther Hollow. Christian agreed to assist with the show and even offered to drive. In preparation for the show, I was careful to pray specific spiritual warfare prayers for protection over myself. After all, it was Halloween, and who knew what we might encounter. I charged my Sony video camera all day to ensure I would have plenty of battery power for anything I might experience.

*666, aka the mark of the beast, painted on a tree. (Panther Hollow)*

Just as before, we first went to the Headless Angel cemetery. While Christian waited in the truck, I approached the cemetery. I stopped outside the gate and shot video into the graveyard. Everything seemed fine at first. Then as soon as I crossed the threshold into the cemetery, the battery warning on my video camera began flashing red. My battery had suddenly drained as soon as I entered the cemetery. I know I had charged the battery all day, and I had plenty of battery power until I stepped into the cemetery. I do consider this to be paranormal because I know demons can drain the batteries of electronic devices and then use that power to manifest. This is an accepted fact among researchers in the paranormal field. With my camera out of commission, we broadcast a little longer from the cemetery and then moved on to Panther Hollow.

*"Death" spelled backwards as practiced and taught by notorious satanist Aleister Crowley. (Panther Hollow)*

*Orbs near a tree marked with a swastika. (Panther Hollow)*

*"We the burned" painted on a tree. (Panther Hollow)*

*This picture shows orbs and an unidentified object moving laterally across frame.*
*(Panther Hollow)*

Upon arrival we found that although it was Halloween, there was no evidence of any rituals. We drove throughout the valley while broadcasting live. The show went well, and as we wrapped things up and headed home, everything seemed to be uneventful...or so we thought.

I had to admit though, I did experience that uncomfortable, familiar feeling after arriving home. Again I prayed, and the feelings dissipated.

# CHAPTER FORTY-TWO

## JANUARY 2013

On January 18, 2013, just three and a half months after our Halloween broadcast from Holmes County, I received a peculiar phone call from Christian.

"Pat, I have something I need to talk to you about, but I don't want you to think I'm crazy," he said.

"Trust me, I won't think you're crazy. What's wrong?" I replied.

Christian took a deep breath and then continued. "Look, like I said, I don't want you to think I'm crazy, but I think something followed me home from Holmes County on Halloween. I've been having some crazy things happening that I can't explain, and it all started after we went there."

"Well, it is possible for demons to attach to you in those types of environments. And I suppose you'd be most vulnerable at a satanic meeting site. Especially on Halloween. Tell me more about what you're experiencing," I replied.

*Filming at the edge of the cemetery. When I crossed to the inside, my camera batteries immediately died. (Headless Angel Cemetery)*

"Pat, it's crazy. Things keep coming up missing. First an important document went missing. I know where it should be, but it's gone. Then I started having cash go missing. I put the cash in a cabinet, and now it's gone. No explanation. Gift cards go missing and then turn up in strange places. Like a Sears gift card went missing and then later turned up behind my desk, but the cardboard packaging was gone. Then someone hit my Jeep, and I had to get a written estimate for the repair. I put the estimate in the armrest, and now it's missing! My stepson lost a tooth, so we gave him money. Now that money is missing, and it was in the same cabinet as the other missing cash," Christian explained.

I was thinking to myself that so far what Christian was telling me could have simply been the result of another family member stealing. As Christian continued, however, those suspicions vanished.

"Sometimes when I'm home alone, I hear doors opening and closing. My dog hears it too and reacts. I'm not imagining this!"

"Christian, I don't think you're imagining it. I believe you. If this is paranormal, and you're experiencing the beginning stages of a haunting, it will often begin just like what you're describing. Then as it progresses, you'll start noticing things like shadows out of the corner of your eye that disappear when you look," I answered.

"Ok. Well, I didn't even get to that yet. I'm already experiencing that! And it all started after I began hearing the doors opening and closing. And there's more. I totaled two vehicles in three weeks in completely freak accidents. The second accident I believe was paranormal. I got in my truck and went to back down the lane, when suddenly it was like I was on a sheet of ice! There was no ice, but I began going backwards down the hill and couldn't stop! I was pushing on the brakes and could see the brake lights, but I wasn't stopping. I just kept going faster. I ended up hitting a tree, and I totaled my truck!" Christian explained.

"It seems like the activity is progressing very quickly, so this needs to be dealt with before it gets worse and someone gets hurt," I replied.

"Well, I guess that's what I need to know. Will you come here and get rid of it? I know you've dealt with this kind of thing before, so I'm hoping you can make it leave."

I thought for a few seconds and then replied, "I can be there Sunday evening if that works for you."

"Yes, Sunday works. Thank you! I appreciate your help," Christian responded.

As I hung up the phone, I thought about the spiritual warfare prayers I'd prayed before and after going to Holmes County on Halloween. I couldn't help but wonder what I might be experiencing in my home if I hadn't done that.

\* \* \*

THE FOLLOWING Sunday with my Bible and anointing oil in hand, I paid Christian a visit. Christian's home was beautiful and quite large, and in a very pretty area near a golf course. As I looked around the home, I couldn't help but think about how easily demonic spirits can attach to us. Now, this beautiful home was housing not only Christian and his family, but something sinister that followed him from Holmes County. Righteous indignation rose in me, and I knew it was time to get to work. I walked throughout the house, praying against the evil spirits and confronting them in the name of Jesus. It was time for them to leave, and I wasn't taking no for an answer. After systematically driving the demons out of the house and back to where they came from, I blessed the house in the name of the Father, Son and Holy Spirit. The house had a tangible peaceful feeling as I wrapped up my work and headed home. Christian later confirmed that the paranormal activity in the house had ceased after my visit.

# CHAPTER FORTY-THREE

## THE PRESS

*A*s I continued researching Holmes County, I remembered that when I was a child, I had seen a newspaper article in the *Times Reporter* that stated the Holmes County sheriff had discovered satanic cult activity in Holmes County. Finding that article seemed impossible, however, because I had no idea the exact year or month I had seen it, and researching microfilm at the local library would be a daunting task. In 2020, however, with the advancements in online newspaper archives, I was able to locate that article. It was dated July 9, 1983. The article described a brutal slaying of a horse, which was decapitated, and its blood was drained and removed from the scene, along with its head. Ironically, the Holmes County Sheriff's Department denied any knowledge of cults in Holmes County. More ironically, the deputy interviewed in this article was Lieutenant Zimmerly, who later became Sheriff Zimmerly, which is who I dealt with during my *Nightmare in Holmes County*. Even back in 1983, the sheriff had turned a blind eye to the blatant cult activity in the county. Or could Zimmerly actually be that oblivious to something so obvious? I think not.

# Was horse in Holmes killed for its blood?

**MILLERSBURG** — An 1,100-pound saddle horse, decapitated July 1 in a pasture on RD 4, may have been the victim of a cult, according to a Holmes County sheriff deputy.

The horse's head was cut off with either a knife or ax between 8:30 a.m. and 7 p.m., said Lt. Tim Zimmerly, and its blood was drained and carried away in buckets. "At least there wasn't any blood there (in the pasture)," said Zimmerly.

The horse's head and neck, and the halter it was wearing, all were taken from the scene. A pickup truck was seen leaving the area that afternoon.

The bizarre aspects of the killing lead lawmen to think it is the work of a cult. However, the incident has not been connected with any group and Zimmerly said he does not know of any cults in the county.

"It's a weird incident, we've never had anything like this before," he added.

The horse was valued at $400.

The owner theorized that the horse's blood was collected in a bucket before the head and neck were cleanly severed from the body. He said there was a ring on the horse's body where the bucket apparently was placed while the blood was being drawn.

*A local newspaper article from July 9, 1983, documented cult activity in Holmes county.*

I stumbled across another article published in another local newspaper, the *Daily Record* from Wooster, Ohio. The article was from October 28, 2007, and was written by staff writer Nick Sabo. In the article Sabo reports on both Panther Hollow and Salem Cemetery, aka the Headless Angel.

Sabo dubs the headless angel gravestone as the "Angel of Death" and acknowledged Panther Hollow as "reputed to be the home of witchcraft ritual sites and ground zero for haunted." In the article Sabo interviewed a township trustee named Lester Yoder as his information source. The following are quotes from the article:

*"Over the years tales of the angel as an agent of death have sprung up. Anyone who met the angel's gaze at midnight was not long for this world."*

*"The angel has been the target of vandals, with the hands and wings smashed. The head was broken off, stolen and subsequently returned at least three times, until it was finally given to the Conrad's descendants by Mechanic Township trustees."* (George and Mary Conrad are buried in the grave marked with the angel statue atop the gravestone.)

*"The angel's morbid powers were not enough to scare away vandals, however. After a spate of vandalism sprees, trustees cut back vegetation and trees near the roadway and installed a security light. The vandals were ruthless, but on at least one occasion the angel had her revenge. Shortly after the head was stolen, police investigating a fatal accident opened the car trunk and saw the angel's fateful faze. 'This young fellow had died in the accident, and when they opened the trunk, there was the head,' Yoder said. 'It turned out he stole the head that night.'"*

*"In the neighborhood of Salem Cemetery is Panther's Hollow, located along County Road 407. The hollow is supposedly the site, past and present, of witchcraft rituals and a 'cry baby' bridge."*

*"Panther's Hollow seems to be one of those spots that has for one reason or another, been associated with enchantment, a place that has always had a spiritual energy."*

# THE CONCLUSION

Years after I was delivered of my *Nightmare in Holmes County*, I happened upon Jonus' son Tim, who had helped build our house in Holmes County. As we talked, Tim told me that he believes that he and his dad unearthed something demonic when they broke ground to build the house. Tim stated that he believes that whatever demonic forces were unleashed caused his father's erratic behavior while building the house, which led to faulty building practices and strife. "Pat, Dad just wasn't himself while we were building your house. I really think that whatever was there was affecting him negatively," Tim stated.

Tim then went on to say that he was aware of the occult activity among the Amish and that he had actually witnessed the Amish conjuring demons out of a bonfire during a rumspringa party. "I could actually see the demons coming up out of the fire," he said.

\* \* \*

Throughout the years since my nightmare ended, I have confirmed that there are satanic meeting sites throughout

Holmes County, including near my former property, in Panther Hollow, and in Mount Hope, among others. Regardless of what many want to believe, Satanism is alive and well among the Amish in Holmes County.

The dark forces I was up against in Holmes County were very real, but I thank God every day that He delivered me. There is evil in this world, and sometimes we have to fight back. But take heart, evil can be defeated through Jesus Christ. I know because I did it.

# ABOUT THE AUTHOR

Patrick Meechan is an author specializing in the subject of spiritual warfare. In addition to *Nightmare in Holmes County*, he also authored *220 Fifth Street*, an Amazon best seller in the categories of Religious Warfare and Satanism. Patrick's unique experiences regarding the demonic realm and exorcism have given him unique insight not often found in the deliverance ministry or the paranormal community.

Printed in Great Britain
by Amazon